Praise for

HAIL, HOLY QUEEN

"In simple and straightforward prose, Dr. Scott Hahn's *Hail, Holy Queen* explains the place of the Blessed Virgin Mary in Christian piety. Eminently readable and insightfully structured, *Hail, Holy Queen* examines and analyzes the biblical and theological foundations of Marian devotion with insight and deep faith." —EDWARD CARDINAL EGAN
Archbishop of New York

"I highly recommend this splendid work of Scott Hahn. I believe that so many people will find *Hail, Holy Queen* very helpful in discovering and rediscovering Mary. The book's style is simple and elegant. Its message, in fidelity to Vatican II, is crystal-clear in concentrating our attention on Mary, the Mother of God, in her relationship to Christ and His Church."
—MOST REVEREND JUSTIN RIGALI
Archbishop of St. Louis

"In his inimitable sparkling style Scott Hahn serves up a feast of Scripture, theology, and spirituality for Christians Catholic and Protestant alike for understanding the role of Mary in God's purposes."
—FR. GEORGE T. MONTAGUE, S.M.
Past President, Catholic Biblical Association; Professor of Scripture, St. Mary's University, San Antonio, Texas

"It is a remarkable presentation of the biblical texts on Mary. They should be the soul of Catholic Mariology and it should help Protestant readers toward a better understanding of Holy Scripture."
—FR. BERTRAND DE MARGERIE, S.J.
French and American Societies of Marian Studies, International Society of Patristic Studies, and Pontifical Roman Academy of St. Thomas Aquinas, Rome

"*Hail, Holy Queen* is a patient and personal development that answers all common objections to Catholic devotion to Mary. Its presentation will convey to the reader both persuasive arguments and excitement for embracing Mary as Mother and Queen."

—FR. MICHAEL SCANLAN, T.O.R.
Chancellor of Franciscan University of Steubenville

"I shall be zealously recommending this book to all and sundry, Catholic *and* Protestant. Scott Hahn is a serious theologian, but his prose may always be counted upon to be agile and lucid. It is difficult to imagine any ground at all from which a rejoinder to his portrait of the Blessed Mother might be mounted."

—THOMAS HOWARD
author of *Lead, Kindly Light, On Being Catholic,*
and *Evangelical Is Not Enough*

HAIL, HOLY QUEEN

The Mother of God in the Word of God

SCOTT HAHN

IMAGE BOOKS • DOUBLEDAY

New York • London • Toronto • Sydney • Auckland

AN IMAGE BOOK
PUBLISHED BY DOUBLEDAY

A hardcover edition of this book was published in 2001 by Doubleday.

Published in the United States by Doubleday, an imprint of The Doubleday Broadway Publishing Group, a division of Random House, Inc., New York.
www.doubleday.com

Book design by Julie Duquet

LIBRARY OF CONGRESS CATALOGING-IN-PUBLICATION DATA
Hahn, Scott.
Hail, Holy Queen: the Mother of God in the word of God / by Scott Hahn.—1st ed.
p. cm.
Includes bibliographical references.
1. Mary, Blessed Virgin, Saint. I. Title.
BT602.H27 2001
232.91—dc21
00-047497

Nihil Obstat: Rev. James Dunfee, Censor Librorum
Imprimatur: Most Rev. Gilbert I. Sheldon, Bishop of Steubenville
The *Nihil Obstat* and *Imprimatur* are official declarations that a book or pamphlet is free of doctrinal or moral error. No implication is contained therein that those who have granted the *Nihil Obstat* and *Imprimatur* agree with the contents, opinions, or statements expressed.

ISBN-13: 978-0-385-50169-9
ISBN-10: 0-385-50169-2

PRINTED IN THE UNITED STATES OF AMERICA

12 14 16 18 20 19 17 15 13

To Hannah

CONTENTS

FOREWORD

by Father Kilian Healy, O.Carm.

A FEW MONTHS BEFORE her death, Saint Thérèse of Lisieux fulfilled her dream to express in song everything she thought about the Blessed Virgin Mary. She entitled her long, twenty-five-stanza poem "Why I Love You, O Mary." Her desire was to tell the truth about Mary, and she draws all her knowledge of Mary, facts and events, from the gospels. For Saint Thérèse, Mary, Mother of God, is her spiritual mother and heavenly queen, but more mother than queen. Among her more than fifty poems, this song of love is considered the favorite by Thérèse's readers and disciples.

Scott Hahn, in *Hail, Holy Queen,* tells us not in poetry but in prose why he loves and honors the Virgin Mary and why we should love and honor her too. While (like Saint Thérèse) he finds Mary's role revealed in the gospels, his search goes beyond them. He is a firm believer in the principle of Saint Augustine that the New Testament is concealed in the Old, and the Old revealed in the New. Not surprisingly, then, he finds Mary foreshadowed in the Old Testament, especially in Eve, the mother of all the living, in the ark of the covenant, and in the queen mother of the Davidic reign.

Moreover, she is the *heavenly* queen, clothed in the sun in the book of Revelation. He finds her too in the Tradition of the Church, especially in the Church fathers and in the dogmas of the Church (which are interpreters of scripture).

Scott Hahn tells his story in a personal and humble way, always conscious of the false interpretations of Marian doctrine and devotion he once held in his youthful anti-Catholic days. In writing this book he has an opportunity to correct them. But his primary motive is to write for all Christians who will listen, especially for his fellow Catholics, for he wants them to appreciate the place of Mary in their lives.

This brings us to a question: will Christians of different denominations listen to him? I am optimistic. In the past, Mary has been for many an obstacle to unity, but in the last thirty years, since the Second Vatican Council, great strides toward unity have been made. Biblical scholars, both Catholic and Protestant, have come together to study scripture. In 1967 the Ecumenical Society of the Blessed Virgin Mary began in England, and included leaders in the Anglican, Catholic, Methodist, and Orthodox Churches. In 1976 the society was founded in Washington, D.C. Members of both societies meet regularly and publish their findings. Vast problems remain unresolved, but some progress has been made and the societies forge ahead with hope and vision. May Mary, the Mother of All Christians and Mother of Unity, take their efforts to heart, intercede to the Holy Spirit, and help bring about the reunion of all Christians.

One final question: how should we approach this book? My own judgment tells me that it would be a mistake to consider this a bedside companion. Its rich content needs to be pondered and digested. It could serve as a textbook for a class in Marian studies. It would be ideal for a Marian study group. With the Bible in one hand and this book in the other, readers could gain interest and enthusiasm from discussions of the scriptural types of Mary and the Church's dogmas. Only through study, reflection, and prayer will these revealed truths lead to an appreciation and love of Mary, mother and queen, and consequently to a love of the God of mercy Who has given her to us.

When Saint Thérèse wrote her song of praise, she gave

her reason in this way: "In you the Almighty has done great things. I want to ponder them and bless Him for them."

Scott Hahn has pondered the wonders God has wrought in Mary, and he wants to share them with us. He invites us to gaze lovingly on our mother and queen. She is the model and exemplar for all her children. One day she will take us by the hand and lead us gently to the Father, the Son, and the Holy Spirit.

May this book, a labor of love, bring forth the response it deserves.

Feast of the Queenship of Mary, August 22, 2000

HAIL, HOLY QUEEN

INTRODUCTION

Every Mother's Son: Confessions of a Marian Prodigal

For all my newfound piety, I was still fifteen years old, and all too conscious of "cool."

Just months before, I'd left behind several years of juvenile delinquency and accepted Jesus as my personal Lord and Savior. My parents, who were not particularly devout Presbyterians, noticed the change in me and heartily approved. If it took religion to keep me out of juvenile detention, so be it.

Zeal for my new faith consumed me, most of the time. But one spring day, I was aware of something else consuming me. I had a stomach bug, with all the unpleasant symptoms. I explained my predicament to my homeroom teacher, who sent me to the school nurse. The nurse, after taking my temperature, told me to lie down while she phoned my mother.

From the conversation I overheard, I could tell I'd be going home. I felt instant relief and dozed off.

I awoke to a sound that cut me like a razor. It was my mother's voice, and it was saturated with maternal pity.

"Ah," she said when she saw me lying there.

Then suddenly it dawned on me. *My mother is taking me home. What if my friends see her leading me out of the school? What if she tries to put her arm around me? I'll be a laughingstock . . .*

Humiliation was on its way. I could already hear the guys jeering at me. *Did you see his mother wiping his forehead?*

If I had been Catholic, I might have recognized the next fifteen minutes as purgatorial. But to my evangelical imagination, they were sheer hell. Though I stared at the ceiling above the nurse's couch, all I could see was a long and unbearable future as "Mama's boy."

I sat up to face a woman approaching me with the utmost pity. Indeed, it was her pity that I found most repugnant. Implicit in every mother's compassion is her "little" child's need—and such littleness and neediness are most definitely not cool.

"Mom," I whispered before she could get a word out. "Do you suppose you could walk out ahead of me? I don't want my friends to see you taking me home."

My mother didn't say a word. She turned and walked out of the nurse's office, out of the school, and straight to her car. From there, she mothered me home, asking how I felt, making sure I went to bed with the usual remedies.

It had been a close call, but I was pretty sure I'd escaped with my cool intact. I drifted off to sleep in almost perfect peace.

It wasn't till that night that I thought about my "cool" again. My father visited my room to see how I was feeling. Fine, I told him. Then he looked gravely at me.

"Scottie," he said, "your religion doesn't mean much if it's all talk. You have to think about the way you treat other people." Then came the clincher: "Don't ever be ashamed to be seen with your mother."

I didn't need an explanation. I could see that Dad was right, and I was ashamed of myself for being ashamed of my mother.

Spiritual Adolescents

Yet isn't that the way it is with many Christians? As He hung dying on the cross, in His last will and testament, Jesus left us a mother. "When Jesus saw His mother and the disciple whom He loved standing near, He said to His mother, 'Woman, behold, your son!' Then He said to the disciple, 'Behold, your mother!' And from that hour the disciple took her into his home" (Jn 19:26–27).

We are His beloved disciples, His younger siblings (see Heb 2:12). His heavenly home is ours, His Father is ours, and His mother is ours. Yet how many Christians are taking her to their homes?

Moreover, how many Christian churches are fulfilling the New Testament prophecy that "all generations" will call Mary "blessed" (Lk 1:48)? Most Protestant ministers—and here I speak from my own past experience—avoid even mentioning the mother of Jesus, for fear they'll be accused of crypto-Catholicism. Sometimes the most zealous members of their congregations have been influenced by shrill anti-Catholic polemics. To them, Marian devotion is idolatry that puts Mary between God and man or exalts Mary at Jesus' expense. Thus, you'll sometimes find Protestant churches named after Saint Paul, Saint Peter, Saint James, or Saint John—but rarely one named for Saint Mary. You'll frequently find pastors preaching on Abraham or David, Jesus' distant ancestors, but almost never hear a sermon on Mary, His mother. Far from calling her blessed, most generations of Protestants live their lives without calling her at all.

This is not just a Protestant problem. Too many Catholics and Orthodox Christians have abandoned their rich heritage of Marian devotions. They've been cowed by the polemics of fundamentalists, shamed by the snickering of dissenting theologians, or made sheepish by well-meaning but misguided ecumenical sensitivities. They're happy to have a mom who prays for them, prepares their meals, and keeps their home; they just wish she'd stay safely out of sight when others are around who just wouldn't understand.

Mary, Mary, Quite Contrary

I too have been guilty of this filial neglect—not only with my earthly mother, but also with my mother in Jesus Christ, the Blessed Virgin Mary. The path of my conversion led me from juvenile delinquency to Presbyterian ministry. All along the way, I had my anti-Marian moments.

My earliest encounter with Marian devotion came when my Grandma Hahn died. She'd been the only Catholic on either side of my family, a quiet, humble, and holy soul. Since I was the only religious one in the family, my father gave me her religious articles when she died. I looked at them with horror. I held her rosary in my hands and ripped it apart, saying, "God, set her free from the chains of Catholicism that have bound her." I meant it, too. I saw the rosary and the Virgin Mary as obstacles that came between Grandma and Jesus Christ.

Even as I slowly approached the Catholic faith—drawn inexorably by the truth of one doctrine after another—I could not make myself accept the Church's Marian teaching.

The proof of her maternity would come, for me, only when I made the decision to let myself be her son. Despite all the powerful scruples of my Protestant training—remember, just a few years before, I had torn apart my Grandma's beads—I took up the rosary one day and began to pray. I prayed for a very personal, seemingly impossible intention. On the next day, I took up the beads again, and the next day and the next. Months passed before I realized that my intention, the seemingly impossible situation, had been reversed since the day I first prayed the rosary. My petition had been granted.

From Here to Maternity

From that moment, I knew my mother. From that moment, I believe, I truly knew my home in the covenant family of God: Yes, Christ was my brother. Yes, He'd taught me to pray, "Our Father." Now, in my heart, I accepted His command to behold *my* mother.

With this book I wish to share that insight—and its unshakable scriptural foundations—with as many Christians as will listen to me, prayerfully, with an open mind. I wish especially to address fellow Roman Catholics, because many of us need to rediscover our mother, discover her for the first time, or perhaps see her with new eyes. For even those who remain faithful to the Mother of God can sometimes do so in a needlessly defensive way—defiantly standing by their mother even though they can make little scriptural sense of their devotions. They cling to a handful of passages from the New Testament as a sort of last Marian resort. These good Catholics—though they do revere their mother—don't fully understand her significance in the divine plan.

For Mary fills the pages of Scripture from the beginning of the first book through the end of the last. She was there, in God's plan, from the beginning of time, just as the apostles were, and the Church, and the Savior, and she will be there at the moment everything is fulfilled. Still, her motherhood is a discovery waiting to be made. While still a Protestant, when I was an aspiring Scripture scholar, I once set myself to researching motherhood and fatherhood in the Bible. I found hundreds of pages of excellent scholarship on fatherhood, patriarchy, paternity, and so on—but only a few paragraphs on motherhood, matriarchy, and maternity.

What's wrong with this picture? Perhaps motherhood is so little understood and appreciated because our mothers are so close to us. Infants, for example, don't even understand that Mother is a separate entity until they are several months old. Some researchers say that children don't fully come to this realization until they are weaned. I'm not sure that we can *ever* distance ourselves psychically from our mothers—though as teenagers we make them walk several paces ahead of us.

Step Up

Let us make this discovery together, then. Let's walk with God's people through the moments of creation and fall and the promise of redemption, from the giving of the Law to the establishment of a kingdom. At every turn we'll find the promise of a homeland, complete with a dazzling queen who is also a mother to her people. At every turn we'll also find the promise of a home, complete with a mother who is also a powerful intercessor for her children. At the most important stage, we will find a *queen mother,* who alone can complete Christ's kingdom and His home.

Even if you feel you must start this journey a few paces behind—at a distance from history's Most Blessed Mother—I beg you to keep walking with me, and with Mary, toward our common destination, our common home in the heavenly Jerusalem.

CHAPTER 1

My Type of Mother

THE LOVING LOGIC OF MARY'S MATERNITY

MOTHERS ARE THE most difficult people to study. They elude our scrutiny. By nature and by definition, they are relational. They can be considered *as mothers* only in their relationship with their children. That is where they focus their attention, and that is where they would focus ours.

Nature keeps mother and child so close as to be almost indistinct as individuals through the first nine months of life. Their bodies are made for each other. During pregnancy, they share the same food, blood, and oxygen. After birth, nature places the child at the mother's breast for nourishment. The newborn's eyes can see only far enough to make eye contact with Mom. The newborn's ears can clearly hear the beating of the mother's heart and the high tones of the female voice. Nature has even made a woman's skin smoother than her husband's, the better to nestle with the sensitive skin of a baby. The mother, body and soul, points beyond herself, to her child.

Yet as close as nature keeps us to our mothers, they remain mysterious to their children. They remain as mysteries. In the words of G. K. Chesterton's Father Brown, "A thing can sometimes be too close to be seen."

As the Mother of God, Mary is the mother par excellence. So, as all mothers are elusive, she will be more so. As all mothers give of themselves, she will give more. As all mothers point beyond themselves, Mary will to a much greater degree.

A true mother, Mary considers none of her glories her own. After all, she points out, she is only doing God's bidding: "Behold, I am the handmaid of the Lord; let it be to me according to your word" (Lk 1:38). Even when she recognizes her superior gifts, she recognizes that they are gifts: "All generations will call me blessed" (Lk 1:48). For her part, Mary's own soul "magnifies" not herself but "the Lord" (Lk 1:46).

How, then, are we to approach this elusive subject, if she must always be relational? How can we begin to study this woman who always deflects attention away from herself and toward her Child?

Let's Get Metaphysical

To understand the Mother of God, we must begin with God. All Mariology, all Marian devotion, must begin with solid theology and firm credal faith. For all that Mary does, and all that she is, flows from her relationship with God and her correspondence to His divine plan. She is His mother. She is His spouse. She is His daughter. She is His handmaid. We cannot begin to know her if we do not, first, have clear notions about *Him*—about God, His providence, and His dealings with His people.

And that's not as easy as some people would lead us to believe. We, after all, are dependent upon language that engages our imagination, that makes invisible things understandable by comparing them to things that we see: God is boundless, like the sky; He is illuminating, like a fire; He is everywhere, like the wind. Or we contrast God's qualities with our own: we are finite, but He is infinite; we are limited in our power, but He is all-powerful.

Analogy and contrast are as far as most people go in their consideration of God—and these are true, as far as they go. Yet they don't go far enough. God is pure spirit, and all our earthly analogies fall far short of describing Him as He really is.

Theology is the way we approach God on His terms rather than our own. Thus, though there's no easy way of going about it, we can't go deep in our faith unless we're willing to take on the task of theology to some degree.

The *ultimate* truth about God cannot be dependent on anything other than God. We cannot define God in terms of something contingent, as in analogies with creation. God does not depend upon creation for His identity. So even His title of creator is something relative and not absolute. Though He *is* eternal and He *is* the creator, He is not the *eternal creator*. Creation is something that takes place in time, and God transcends time. So, though creation is something God *does,* it does not define Who He is. The same goes for redemption and sanctification. Though God is redeemer and sanctifier, these titles do not define His eternal identity, but rather certain of His works. The terms "creator," "redeemer," "lawgiver," and "sanctifier" are all dependent upon the world—upon something that needs to be created, redeemed, ruled, and sanctified.

What's-His-Name

Then how can we know God as He is? Primarily because He has revealed Himself to us. He has told us

His eternal identity. His *name*. At the end of Saint Matthew's gospel (28:19), Jesus commands His disciples to baptize "in the name" of the Blessed Trinity: the Father, the Son, and the Holy Spirit. Notice that He does not speak of these as three *titles*, but as a single *name*. In the culture of ancient Israel, one's name was equivalent to one's identity. This single name, then, reveals Who God is from all eternity. He is Father, Son, and Holy Spirit.

Now, you might reasonably object, those titles are dependent on creation. Are not "Father" and "Son" mere analogies with earthly familial roles?

No. In fact, that's precisely backwards. Rather, the earthly roles of father and son are living metaphors for something divine and eternal. God Himself is, somehow, eternally, perfectly a family. Pope John Paul II expressed this well: "God in His deepest mystery is not a solitude, but a family, since He has in Himself fatherhood, sonship, and the essence of the family, which is love."

Did you catch that? God, then, is not *like* a family; God *is* a family. From eternity, God alone possesses the essential attributes of a family, and the Trinity alone possesses them in their perfection. Earthly households have these attributes, but imperfectly.

Divinity Is As Divinity Does

Yet God's transcendence does not leave creation completely without a clue. Creation does tell us something about its creator. Artwork always reveals a hint of the character of the artist. So we can learn more about Who God is by observing what He does.

The process works in reverse as well. We can learn more about creation, redemption, and the works of God by studying them in the light of His self-revelation. Because the Trinity reveals the deepest dimension of Who God is, it also reveals the deepest meaning of what God does. The mystery of the Trinity is "the central mystery of Christian faith and life," says the *Catechism of the Catholic Church* (no. 234). "It is the mystery of God in Himself. It is therefore the source of all the other mysteries of faith, the light that enlightens them." Thus, our understanding of God as family should also profoundly affect our understanding of all His works. In everything that exists, we may discern—with the eyes of faith—a familial purpose, what the theological tradition calls "the footprints of the Trinity."

Reflection on the mystery of God and the mysteries of creation, then, becomes mutually enhancing. Says the *Catechism:* "God's works reveal Who He is in Himself; the mystery of His inmost being enlightens our understanding of all His works. So it is, analogously, among human persons. A person discloses himself in his actions, and the better we know a person, the better we understand his actions" (no. 236).

Traces of Love, Long Ago

We catch glimpses of God not just in the world but also—and especially—in the scriptures, which are uniquely inspired by God to convey His truth. The *Catechism* goes on to explain that God has revealed "His Trinitarian being" explicitly in the New Testament, but also left "traces . . . in His Revelation throughout the Old Testament" (no. 237).

The whole of the scriptures, then, can be viewed as the story of God's preparation for, and completion of, His greatest work: His definitive self-revelation in Jesus Christ. Saint Augustine said that the New Testament is concealed in the Old, and the Old is revealed in the New. For all history was the world's preparation for the moment when the Word was made flesh, when God became a human child in the womb of a young virgin from Nazareth.

Like Jesus Christ, the Bible is unique. For it is the only book that can truly claim to have both human authors and a divine author, the Holy Spirit. Jesus Christ is the

Word of God incarnate, fully divine yet fully human—like all of us, except without sin. The Bible is the Word of God inspired, fully divine yet fully human—like any other book, except without error. Both Christ and scripture are given, said the Second Vatican Council, "for the sake of our salvation" (*Dei Verbum* 11).

So when we read the Bible, we need to read it on two levels at once. We read the Bible in a *literal* sense as we read any other human literature. But we read it also in a *spiritual* sense, searching out what the Holy Spirit is trying to tell us through the words (see *Catechism,* nos. 115–19).

We do this in imitation of Jesus, because this is the way He read the scriptures. He referred to Jonah (Mt 12:39), Solomon (Mt 12:42), the temple (Jn 2:19), and the brazen serpent (Jn 3:14) as "signs" that prefigured Him. We see in Luke's gospel, as our Lord comforted the disciples on the road to Emmaus, that "beginning with Moses and all the prophets, He interpreted to them what referred to Him in all the scriptures" (Lk 24:27). After this spiritual reading of the Old Testament, we are told, the disciples' hearts burned within them.

What ignited this fire in their hearts? Through the scriptures, Jesus had initiated His disciples into a world that reached beyond their senses. A good teacher, God introduced the unfamiliar in terms of the familiar. Indeed, He had created the familiar with this end in mind, fashioning the persons and institutions that would best prepare us for the coming of Christ and the glories of His kingdom.

Learning to Type

The first Christians followed their Master in reading the Bible this way. In the letter to the Hebrews, the Old Testament tabernacle and its rituals are described as "types and shadows of heavenly realities" (8:5), and the law as a "shadow of the good things to come" (10:1). Saint Peter, in turn, noted that Noah and his family "were saved through water," and that "this prefigured baptism, which saves you now" (1 Pt 3:20–21). Peter's word translated as "prefigured" is actually the Greek word for "typify," or "make a type." The apostle Paul, for his part, described Adam as a "type" of Jesus Christ (Rom 5:14).

So what is a type? A type is a real person, place, thing, or event in the Old Testament that foreshadows something greater in the New Testament. From "type" we get the word "typology," the study of Christ's foreshadowing in the Old Testament (see *Catechism,* 128–130).

Again, we must emphasize that types are not fictional symbols. They are literally true historical details. When

Saint Paul interpreted the story of Abraham's sons as "an allegory" (Gal 4:24), for example, he was not suggesting that the story never really happened; he was affirming it as history, but as history with a place in God's plan, history whose meaning was clear only after its eventual fulfillment.

Typology unveils more than the person of Christ; it also tells us about heaven, the Church, the apostles, the Eucharist, the places of Jesus' birth and death, and the person of Jesus' mother. From the first Christians we learn that the Jerusalem temple foreshadowed the heavenly dwelling of the saints in glory (2 Cor 5:1–2; Rev 21:9–22); that Israel prefigured the Church (Gal 6:16); that the twelve Old Testament patriarchs prefigured the twelve New Testament apostles (Lk 22:30); and that the ark of the covenant was a type of the Blessed Virgin Mary (Rev 11:19; 12:1–6,13–17).

In addition to Old Testament types *explicitly* discussed in the New Testament, there are many more that are *implicit* but obvious. For example, Saint Joseph's role in the early life of Jesus clearly follows the patriarch Joseph's role in the early life of Israel. The two men share the same name; both are described as "righteous," or "just"; both receive revelations in dreams; both find themselves exiled to Egypt; and both arrive on the scene in order to prepare the way for a greater event—in the patriarch Joseph's case, the exodus led by Moses, the Deliverer; in Saint Joseph's case, the redemption brought about by Jesus, the Redeemer.

Marian types abound in the Old Testament. We find Mary prefigured in Eve, the mother of all the living; in Sarah, the wife of Abraham, who conceived her child miraculously; in the queen mother of Israel's monarchy, who interceded with the king on behalf of the people of the land; and in many other places, in many other ways (for example, Hannah and Esther). The type addressed most explicitly in the New Testament, the ark of the covenant, I will discuss in greater detail in its own chapter. Here I will merely point out that, as the ancient ark was made to bear the old covenant, so the Virgin Mary was created to bear the new covenant.

Family Affairs

It is that new covenant, borne into the world by the Blessed Virgin Mary, that has made all the difference in our lives—in my life and yours—and in human history. For covenants mark all the decisive encounters between God and man. God's relationship with Israel was defined by a covenant, as were His relationships with Adam, Noah, Abraham, Moses, and David. Jesus Himself spoke of His redemptive sacrifice as the new covenant in His blood (Lk 22:20).

We hear those words in the Eucharistic prayer at every Mass, but do we ever pause to ask: what is a covenant? This is a most crucial question, one that brings us to the heart of Christian faith and life. In fact, it brings us to the very heart of God.

What is a covenant? The question leads us back to the primal reality we discussed earlier in this chapter: the family. In the ancient Near East, a covenant was a sacred kinship bond based on a solemn oath that brought someone into a *family* relationship with another person or tribe. When God made His covenants with Adam, Noah, Abraham, Moses, and David, He was gradually inviting a wider circle of people into His family: first a couple, then a family, then a nation, and eventually the world.

All of those covenants failed, however, because of man's unfaithfulness and sin. God remained constantly faithful; Adam did not, and neither did Moses, neither did David. In fact, sacred history leads us to conclude that *only God* keeps His covenant promises. How, then, could mankind fulfill the human end of a covenant in a way that would last forever? That would require a man to be sinless and as constant as God. Thus, for the new and everlasting covenant, God became man in Jesus Christ, and He established the covenant by which we become part of His family: the family of God.

This means more than mere fellowship with God. For "God in His deepest mystery is . . . *a family*." God Himself is Father, Son, and the Spirit of Love—and Christians are drawn up into the life of *that family*. In baptism we are identified with Christ, baptized in the Trinitarian name of God; we take on His family name, and thus we become sons in the Son. We are taken up into the very life of the Trinity, where we may live in love forever. If God is family, heaven is home; and with Jesus, heaven has come to earth.

The Most Functional Family

God's covenant family is perfect, lacking nothing. The Church looks to God as Father, Jesus as Brother, and heaven as home. What's missing, then?

In truth, nothing. Every family needs a mother; only Christ could choose His own, and He chose providentially for His entire covenant family. Now, everything He has He shares with us. His divine life is ours; His home is our home; His Father is our Father; His brothers are our brothers; and His mother is our mother, too.

For a family is incomplete without a loving mother. The breakaway Christian churches that diminish Mary's role inevitably end up feeling like a bachelor's apartment: masculine to a fault; orderly but not homey; functional and productive—but with little sense of beauty and poetry.

Yet all the scriptures, all the types, all creation, and our deepest human needs tell us that no family should be that way—and certainly not the covenant family of God. The apostles knew this, and that's why they were gathered along with Mary in Jerusalem at Pentecost. The early generations of Christians knew this, and that's why they painted her image in their catacombs and dedicated their churches to her.

In the earliest icons of Mary, she is almost always portrayed holding her infant child—forever bearing Him to the world, as in the twelfth chapter of the book of Revelation. A true mother, she is usually portrayed pointing to her son but looking out toward the viewers, her other children. She mothers her infant—for an infant cannot hold himself up—even as she mothers her children in the world and draws us together to Him.

CHAPTER 2

Christmas's Eve

Mary's Motherhood Is Eden Revisited

THE EARLY CHRISTIANS had a lively devotion to the Blessed Virgin. We find evidence of this in their surviving literature and artwork and, of course, in the New Testament, which was their foundational document. While the Mariology of the first three centuries was at a primitive stage of development (compared to that of a later age, or even our own), it was perhaps more consciously scriptural than many later expressions, and more consistently presented in the theological context of creation, fall, incarnation, and redemption. So it sometimes can speak to us with greater clarity, immediacy, and force. For Mary's role makes no sense apart from its context in salvation history; yet it is not incidental to God's plan. God chose to make His redemptive act inconceivable without her.

Mary was in His plan from the very beginning, chosen and foretold from the moment God created man and woman. In fact, the early Christians understood Mary and Jesus to be a reprise of God's first creation. Saint Paul spoke of Adam as a type of Jesus (Rom 5:14) and of Jesus as the new Adam, or the "last Adam" (1 Cor 15:21–22, 45–49).

The early Christians considered the beginning of Genesis—with its story of creation and fall and its promise of redemption—to be so christological in its implications that they called it the *Protoevangelium,* or First Gospel. While this theme is explicit in Paul and the Church Fathers, it is implied throughout the New Testament. For example, like Adam, Jesus was tested in a garden—the garden of Gethsemane (Mt 26:36–46, Jn 18:1). Like Adam, Jesus was led to a "tree," where He was stripped naked (Mt 27:31). Like Adam, He fell into the deep sleep of death, so that from His side would come forth the New Eve (Jn 19:26–35; 1 Jn 5:6–8), His bride, the Church.

Cutting the Unbiblical Cord

The motif of the New Adam is nowhere so artfully developed as in the Gospel according to Saint John. John does not work out the ideas as a commentator would. Instead, he tells the story of Jesus Christ. Yet he begins the story by echoing the most primeval story of all: the story of creation in Genesis.

The most obvious echo comes "in the beginning." Both books, Genesis and John's gospel, in fact, begin with those words. The book of Genesis sets out with the words "In the beginning God created the heavens and the earth" (Gen 1:1). John follows closely, telling us, "In the beginning was the Word, and the Word was with God" (Jn 1:1). In both cases, we are talking about a fresh start, a new creation.

The next echo comes soon afterward. In Genesis 1:3–5, we see that God created the light to shine in the darkness. In John 1:4–5, we see that the Word's "life was the *light* of men" and it "shines in the darkness."

Genesis shows us, in the beginning, "the Spirit of God . . . moving over the face of the waters" (Gen 1:2). John, in turn, shows us the Spirit hovering above the waters of baptism (Jn 1:32–33). At that point, we begin to see the source of the new creation recounted by John. Material creation came about when God breathed His Spirit above the waters. The renewal of creation would come with the divine life given in the waters of baptism.

Counting the Days

John the Evangelist continues to leave hints of Genesis throughout his opening narrative. After the first vignette, John's story continues "the next day" (1:29), with the encounter of Jesus and John the Baptist. "The next day" (1:35), again, comes the story of the calling of the first disciples. "The next day" (1:43), yet again, we find Jesus' call to two more disciples. So, taking John's first discussion of the Messiah as the first day, we now find ourselves on the fourth day.

Then John does something remarkable. He introduces his next episode, the story of the wedding feast at Cana, with the words "On the third day." Now, he cannot mean the third day from the beginning, since he has already proceeded past that point in his narrative. He must mean the third day from the fourth day, which brings us to the seventh day—and then John stops counting days.

Do you notice anything familiar? John's story of the new creation takes place in seven days, just as the creation story in Genesis is completed on the sixth day, and sanctified—perfected—on the seventh, when God rests from His labor. The seventh day of the creation week, as of every week thereafter, would be known as the Sabbath, the day of rest, the sign of the covenant (see Ex

31:16–17). We can be sure, then, that whatever happens on the seventh day in John's narrative will be significant.

I Beg to Defer

Jesus arrives at the wedding feast with His mother and His disciples. A wedding celebration, in the Jewish culture of the time, normally lasted about a week. Yet we find, at this wedding, that the wine ran out very early. At which point, Jesus' mother points out the obvious: "They have no wine" (Jn 2:3). It is a simple statement of fact. But Jesus seems to respond in a way that is far out of proportion to His mother's simple observation. "O woman," he says, "what have you to do with Me? My hour has not yet come."

In order for us to understand Jesus' seeming overreaction, we need to understand the phrase "what have you to do with me?" Some commentators claim that this represents Jesus' brusque reproach of His mother. However, that does not hold up to careful study.

First, we should note that in the end, Jesus does fulfill the request He infers from Mary's observation. If He intended to reproach her, he surely would not have followed His reproach by complying with her request.

The decisive evidence against the reproach reading,

however, comes from the alleged reproach itself. "What have you to do with me?" was a common Hebrew and Greek idiom in Jesus' day. It is found in several other places in the Old and New Testaments, as well as in sources outside the Bible. In all other occurrences, it certainly does *not* signify reproach or disrespect. Quite the opposite: it conveys respect and even deference. Consider Luke 8:28, when the line is used verbatim by a man possessed by a devil. It is the demon who puts those words in the possessed man's mouth, and he means them to acknowledge Jesus' authority over both the man and the demon. "I beseech you, do not torment me," he continues, thereby affirming that he must carry out whatever Jesus commands.

At Cana, Jesus defers to His mother, though she never commands Him. She, in turn, merely tells the servants, "Do whatever He tells you" (Jn 2:5).

Daughter-Mother-Bride: Woman

But let's return for a moment to Jesus' initial response. Did you notice how He addressed her? He called her not "Mother" or even "Mary," but "Woman." Again, non-Catholic commentators will sometimes claim that Jesus intended the epithet "Woman" to convey disrespect or reproach. After all, shouldn't He address her as "Mother"?

First, we should point out that since Jesus was obedient all His life to the law, it is unlikely that He would ever show dishonor to His mother, thereby violating the fourth commandment.

Second, Jesus will again address Mary as "Woman," but in very different circumstances. As He hangs dying on the cross, He will call her "Woman" when He gives her *as mother* to His beloved disciple, John (Jn 19:26). Surely, in that instance, He could mean no reproach or dishonor.

Yet we miss more than Jesus' sinlessness if we reduce the word "woman" to an insult. For Jesus' use of that word represents yet another echo of Genesis. "Woman" is the name Adam gives to Eve (Gen 2:23). Jesus, then, is addressing Mary as Eve to the New Adam—which heightens the significance of the wedding feast they're attending.

Still, we can anticipate some outraged objection: how can Mary be His bride if she's His mother? To answer that, we must consider Isaiah's prophecy of the coming salvation of Israel: "You shall no more be termed Forsaken . . . but you shall be called My Delight Is in Her, and your land Married. For *as a young man marries a virgin, so shall your sons marry you, and as the bridegroom rejoices over the bride, so shall your God rejoice over you"* (Is 62:4–5; italics added). There's a lot suggested in those two compact verses: Mary's virginal motherhood, her miraculous conception, and her mystical marriage to God, who is at once her Father, her Spouse, and her Son. The mystery of divine maternity runs deep, because the mystery of the Trinity runs still deeper.

Maternity Warred

"Woman" redefines Mary's relationship not only with Jesus but also with all believers. When Jesus gave her over to His beloved disciple, in effect He gave her to His beloved disciples of all time. Like Eve, whom Genesis 3:20 calls "mother of all the living," Mary is mother to all who have new life in baptism.

At Cana, then, the New Eve radically reverses the fatal decision of the first Eve. It was woman who led the old Adam to his first evil act in the garden. It was woman who led the New Adam to His first glorious work.

The figure of Eve reappears later in the New Testament, in the book of Revelation, which is also attributed to John the Evangelist. There, in chapter 12, we encounter "a woman clothed with the sun" (v. 1), who confronts "the ancient serpent, who is called the devil" (v. 9). These images hark back to Genesis, where Eve faces the demonic serpent in the garden of Eden and where God curses the serpent, promising to "put enmity between you and the woman, and between your seed and her seed" (Gen 3:15). Yet the images of Revelation also point to a New Eve, one who gave birth to a "male child" who would "rule all the nations" (12:5). That child could only be Jesus; and so the woman could only be His mother, Mary. In Revelation, the ancient serpent attacks the New Eve because the prophecy of Genesis 3:15 is fresh in his memory. The New Eve, however, appears prevailing over evil, unlike her long-ago type in the garden of Eden.

Justin Time

The parallels between the gospel of John and Genesis are striking. Still, I know that some skeptics will dismiss them as the product of an overexcited imagination. Have we Catholics, perhaps, read too much into John's text? Are we just imposing medieval and modern doctrines onto an author who would never have dreamt them up?

Those are fair questions. We begin by investigating evidence from the early Christians, beginning in the circles closest to the apostle John. As we study these earliest fathers of the Church, we find that they did indeed speak of a New Eve. Who did they say she was? Overwhelmingly, they identified her as Mary.

The earliest surviving testimony to this is in Saint

Justin Martyr's *Dialogue with Trypho.* Written around 160, the *Dialogue* describes conversations Justin had had with a rabbi around 135 in Ephesus, the city where Justin was instructed in the Christian faith. According to tradition, Ephesus was also the city where the apostle John lived with the Virgin Mary.

Justin's doctrine of the New Eve resonates with that of John himself, and may be evidence of a Mariology developed by John as bishop of Ephesus and continued by his disciples in Justin's day—which was little more than a generation after the apostle's death.

Justin's statement is compact, but rich:

> *Christ became man by the Virgin, in order that the disobedience that proceeded from the serpent might receive its destruction in the same manner in which it derived its origin. For Eve, who was a virgin and undefiled, having conceived the word of the serpent, brought forth disobedience and death. But the Virgin Mary received faith and joy when the angel Gabriel announced the good tidings to her that the Spirit of the Lord would come upon her, and the power of the Highest would overshadow her: wherefore also the Holy Thing begotten of her is the Son of God; and she replied, "Be it unto me according to Thy word" (Lk 1:38). And by her has He been born, to Whom we*

have proved so many Scriptures refer, and by Whom God destroys both the serpent and those angels and men who are like him.

In comparing and contrasting Eve with Mary, Justin follows Paul's discussions of Christ and Adam. Paul points out that "in Adam all die," while "in Christ shall all be made alive" (1 Cor 15:22). "Adam became a living being," while "the last Adam became a life-giving spirit" (1 Cor 15:45). Adam passed on our mortal and earthly family resemblance; but Christ made us part of an immortal and heavenly family (1 Cor 15:49).

Justin, in turn, notes that Eve and Mary were both virgins; Eve conceived the "word of the serpent," while Mary conceived the Word of God. By God's providence, Justin concludes, Mary's obedience became a means of undoing Eve's disobedience and its most devastating effects.

The Lyons Den

The Marian paper trail continues from Justin to Saint Irenaeus of Lyons, who further refined the Church's understanding of Mary as the New Eve. Irenaeus, too, could trace his pedigree as a disciple back to the apostle John. Irenaeus learned the faith from Saint Polycarp of Smyrna, who himself took instruction from John. Perhaps, again, it was the influence of John that led Irenaeus to speak of Christ as the New Adam and Mary as the New Eve, as he did in several places.

The doctrine, in fact, was essential to one of Irenaeus's central ideas: what he called creation's *recapitulation* in Christ. Building on Saint Paul, he wrote that when Christ "became incarnate, and was made man, He recapitulated in Himself the long history of man, summing up and giving us salvation in order that we might receive again in Christ Jesus what we had lost in Adam—that is, the image and likeness of God."

Like John, Irenaeus saw the important place of the New Eve in this recapitulation. "The knot of Eve's disobedience was loosed by the obedience of Mary. The knot which the virgin Eve tied by her unbelief, the Virgin Mary opened by her belief." In the subsequent paragraphs, Irenaeus contrasts Mary's obedience with Eve's disobedience, analyzing the scriptural texts.

In a later book, he developed the idea further: "If the former [Eve] disobeyed God, the latter [Mary] was persuaded to obey God, so that the Virgin Mary became the advocate of the virgin Eve. And thus, as the human race fell into bondage to death by means of a virgin, so it is rescued by a virgin." Here, Irenaeus's discussion of Mary as advocate (which he takes up again in his *Proof of the Apostolic Preaching*) suggests, to this reader at least, her intercessory power at Cana.

Finally, Irenaeus extends Mary's maternity from Christ to all Christians, as he speaks of her as a type of the Church. He describes Jesus' birth as "the pure one opening purely that pure womb which regenerates men unto God."

Out of Africa

Justin in Ephesus and Irenaeus in France might both claim spiritual descent from the apostle John. John himself taught from a mighty experience; for he had lived for three years beside Jesus and then, in the following years, in the same home as the Virgin Mary. Cardinal John Henry Newman reflected:

> *If there is an apostle on whom our eyes would be fixed, as likely to teach us about the Blessed Virgin, it is St. John, to whom she was committed by our Lord on the cross—with whom, as tradition goes, she lived at Ephesus till she was taken away. This anticipation is confirmed; for, as I have said above, one of the earliest and fullest of our in-*

formants concerning her dignity, as being the Second Eve, is Irenaeus, who came to Lyons from Asia Minor and had been taught by the immediate disciples of St. John.

Yet there were others, possibly outside John's direct line of influence, who saw Mary as the New Eve. Tertullian—in North Africa at the beginning of the third century—spoke of this reality with precision:

For it was while Eve was yet a virgin that the ensnaring word had crept into her ear which was to build the edifice of death. Into a virgin's soul, in like manner, must be introduced that Word of God which was to raise the fabric of life; so that what had been reduced to ruin by this sex might by the selfsame sex be recovered to salvation. As Eve believed the serpent, so Mary believed the angel. The delinquency which the one occasioned by believing, the other effaced by believing.

His precision is all the more remarkable considering that his Mariology, in other areas, is quite confused, erring, and at odds with all other sources.

The New Eve, then, is hardly a medieval or modern innovation in reading the gospel. Rather, it is an ancient and sacred tradition passed—probably from the apostle

John himself—down through the ages, to be taught by Saint Justin, Saint Irenaeus, Tertullian, Saint Augustine, Saint John Damascene, Saint Thomas Aquinas, and many thousands of others.

All those teachers clearly discerned the message of the New Eve. It is this: Obey God, Who is her Son, her Spouse, her Father. "Do whatever He tells you." The medieval poets summed it up neatly by pointing out that the angel Gabriel's *Ave* (the Latin greeting) reversed the name of *Eva*. So also did it reverse the rebellious inclination Eve left to her children—to you and me—and replace it with the readiness to obey, which Mary wants to teach us.

CHAPTER 3

Venerators of the Lost Ark

Israel and the Bearer of the New Covenant

WHAT WE GLIMPSE in shadows in John's gospel we find "clothed with the sun" in John's Apocalypse, the book of Revelation. Even the title of that last book of the Bible leads us back to John's gospel. "Revelation" is the usual English rendering of the Greek *apokalypsis;* but the Greek word is richer than that. It is more accurately translated as "unveiling," and was used by Greek-speaking Jews to describe the moment when the bride was unveiled before her husband, just before the couple consummated their marriage.

So, once again, as at Cana, we find ourselves with John at a wedding feast. John writes in Revelation: "Blessed are those who are invited to the marriage supper of the Lamb" (Rev 19:9). Now, throughout the Apocalypse,

John uses "the Lamb" to denote Jesus. But who is the bride at this wedding? Toward the end of the book, an angel takes John and tells him, "Come, I will show you the bride, the wife of the Lamb." Then, together, they see "the holy city Jerusalem coming down out of heaven from God" (Rev 21:9–10). Jerusalem, it seems, is the bride of Christ. Yet the Jerusalem John describes looks nothing like the earthly Jerusalem. Instead, it shines with "radiance like a most rare jewel. . . . The foundations of the wall of the city are adorned with every jewel. . . . The twelve gates are twelve pearls, each of the gates made of a single pearl, and the street of the city is pure gold, transparent as glass" (Rev 21:11,19,21).

Those are beautiful images, but they hardly describe a real city—never mind a bride. What or who, then, is this holy city that is also a bride? Most interpreters, both ancient and modern, believe that the holy city is the Church, depicted by John as the New Jerusalem; for Saint Paul also speaks of the Church in a bridal relationship with Christ (Eph 5:31–32).

Yet if that were all John needed to reveal to us, his Apocalypse would have been a much shorter book. Instead, it is twenty-two chapters long, and filled with images that are sometimes dazzling, sometimes frightening, and often puzzling. We don't have the space here for a full-scale study of the book of Revelation; but I would like to focus on one of its culminating scenes, its first "unveiling," which takes place midway through the book.

Ark the Herald Angels Sing

To Jews of the first century, the shocker in the Apocalypse was surely John's disclosure at the end of chapter 11. It is then that, after hearing seven trumpet blasts, John sees the heavenly temple opened (Rev 11:19) and within it—a miracle!—the ark of the covenant.

This would have been the news story of the millennium. The ark of the covenant—the holiest object in ancient Israel—had been missing for *six centuries.* Around 587 B.C., the prophet Jeremiah concealed the ark in order to preserve it from defilement when Babylonian invaders came to destroy the temple. We can read the story in 2 Maccabees:

> *Jeremiah came and found a cave, and he brought there the tent and the ark and the altar of incense, and he sealed up the entrance. Some of those who followed him came up to mark the way, but could not find it. When Jeremiah learned of it, he rebuked them and declared: "The place shall be unknown until God gathers His people together*

again and shows His mercy. And then the Lord will disclose these things, and the glory of the Lord and the cloud will appear." (2 Mac 2:5–8)

When Jeremiah speaks of "the cloud," he means the *shekinah*, or glory cloud, that shrouded the ark of the covenant and signified God's presence. Within Solomon's temple, the ark had occupied the holy of holies. In fact, the ark was what *made* that inner sanctum holy. For the ark held the tablets of stone on which the finger of God had traced the ten commandments. The ark contained a relic of the manna, the food God gave to sustain His people during their desert sojourn. The ark also preserved Aaron's rod, the symbol of his priestly office.

Made of acacia wood, the ark was box shaped, covered with gold ornament, and overshadowed by carved cherubim. Atop the ark was the mercy seat, which was always unoccupied. Standing before the ark, within the Holy Place, stood the menorah, or seven-branched candlestick.

Yet the first Jewish readers of the Apocalypse knew these details only from history and tradition. Since Jeremiah's hiding place had never been found, the rebuilt temple had no ark in its holy of holies, no *shekinah*, no manna in the ark, and no cherubim or mercy seat.

Then along came John claiming to have seen the *shekinah* (the "glory of God," Rev 21:10–11,23)—and most remarkable of all, the ark of the covenant.

Mary Had a Little Lamb

John prepares his reader in many ways for the appearance of the ark. The ark appears, for example, after the blare of the seventh trumpet of the seventh avenging angel. This is a clear allusion to Israel of the old covenant. In the first and greatest battle that Israel fought upon entering the promised land, God commanded the chosen people to carry the ark before them into the fray. Specifically, Revelation 11:15 echoes Joshua 6:13, which describes how, for six days leading up to the Battle of Jericho, Israel's seven warrior priests marched around the city with the ark of the covenant before, on the seventh day, they blew their trumpets, bringing down the city walls. For ancient Israel, the ark was, in a sense, the most effective weapon, for it represented the protection and power of almighty God. Likewise, Revelation shows that the new and heavenly Israel also does battle in the presence of the ark.

As we might expect, the ark appears with spectacular special effects: "Then God's temple in heaven was opened, and the ark of His covenant was seen within His temple; and there were flashes of lightning, voices, peals of thunder, an earthquake, and heavy hail" (Rev 11:19).

Imagine that you are a first-century reader, raised as a Jew. You have never seen the ark, but all your religious and cultural upbringing has taught you to long for its restoration in the temple. John builds anticipation, so that he almost seems to be teasing such readers by describing the sound and fury accompanying the ark. The dramatic tension becomes nearly unbearable. The reader wants to *see* the ark, as John sees it.

What follows, then, is jarring. In our contemporary Bibles, after all that buildup, the passage suddenly comes to a screeching halt as chapter 11 concludes. John promises us the ark, but then seems to bring his scene to an abrupt end. We must keep in mind, however, that the chapter divisions in Revelation—as in all the books of the Bible—are artificial, imposed by scribes in the Middle Ages. There were no chapters in John's original Apocalypse; it was one continuous narrative.

Thus the special effects at the end of chapter 11 served as an *immediate* prelude for the image that now appears at the beginning of chapter 12. We can read those lines together as describing a single event: "Then God's temple in heaven was opened, and the ark of His covenant was seen. . . . A great portent appeared in heaven, a woman clothed with the sun, with the moon under her feet, and on her head a crown of twelve stars; she was with child and she cried out in her pangs of birth, in anguish for delivery" (Rev 11:19–12:2).

John has shown us the ark of the covenant—and it is a woman.

The Apocalypse can indeed seem strange. Earlier we saw a bride that appeared as a city; now we see an ark that appears as a woman.

Battle Lines

Who is this woman who is also an ark? Most commentators agree that, on one level at least, this woman—like the bride of Revelation 19—represents the Church, which labors to give birth to believers in every age. Yet it is unlikely that John intended the woman exclusively, or even primarily, to represent the Church. Cardinal Newman offered one compelling argument why personification does not suffice as a reading of Revelation 12:

> *The image of the woman, according to general Scripture usage, is too bold and prominent for a mere personification. Scripture is not fond of allegories. We have indeed frequent figures there, as when the sacred writers speak of the arm or sword of the Lord. So, too, when they speak of Jerusalem*

> *or Samaria in the feminine, or of the Church as a bride or as a vine. But they are not much given to dressing up abstract ideas or generalizations in personal attributes. This is the classical rather than the scriptural style. Xenophon places Hercules between Virtue and Vice, represented as women.*

Indeed, mere personification doesn't seem to fit John's method throughout the episode with the woman. For he introduces other fantastic characters, who may embody certain ideas, but there can be no doubt that they are also real persons. For example, few interpreters question the identity of the "male child" the woman brings forth (Rev 12:5). Given the context in Revelation, this male child could only be Jesus Christ. John tells us the child "is to rule all the nations with a rod of iron," and this clearly is a reference to Psalm 2:9, which describes the messianic king promised by God. John also adds that this child "was caught up to God and to His throne," which can only refer to Jesus, who ascended into heaven.

What is true for the male child is also true for His enemy, the dragon. John states plainly that the dragon is not only an allegory but a specific person: "that ancient serpent, who is called the Devil and Satan, the deceiver of the whole world" (Rev 12:9).

In the same way, the dragon's ally, the "beast rising out of the sea" (Rev 13:1), also corresponds to real people. Let's look at that hideous beast and then look back into history, to see what John saw. The beast has "ten horns and seven heads, with ten crowns upon its horns and a blasphemous name upon its heads." We know from chapter 7 of the book of Daniel that in prophecy, such beasts usually represent dynasties. Horns, for example, are a common symbol of dynastic power.

We should ask ourselves, then: in the first century, which dynasty was most threatened by the rise of the messianic king from David's line? Matthew's gospel (chapter 2) makes that clear: it was the dynasty of Herod, the Herodians. Herod, after all, was a non-Jew, appointed by the Romans to rule Judea. In order to shore up his illegitimate reign, the Romans wiped out all heirs of the Jews' Hasmonean dynasty. Yet Herod claimed to be king in Jerusalem, and even went so far as to rebuild the temple on a grand scale. A charismatic leader, Herod—even though he was a gentile—earned, by turns, the fear, gratitude, and even worship of his subjects throughout his bloody reign. This first of the Herods murdered his own wife, three of his sons, his mother-in-law, a brother-in-law, and an uncle, not to mention all the infants of Bethlehem.

Moreover, Herod had insinuated the temple priests into his governance. Whom did Herod consult, after all, when he sought the newborn Messiah? The Herodian dynasty, then, was a satanic counterfeit of the House of David. Like David's true heir, Solomon, Herod had built up the temple and kept multiple wives. He had also, with help from the Romans, unified the land of Israel as it had not been in centuries.

The Herods would make themselves the greatest obstacle to the true restoration of David's kingdom. Seven Herods ruled in the line of the founding father, Antipater, and there were ten Caesars in Rome's imperial line from Julius to Vespasian. The beast with ten horns and seven heads corresponds rather curiously to the seven crowned Herods who drew their power to rule from the dynasty of the ten Caesars.

To claim that Revelation 12 is an exercise in personification would be a gross oversimplification. John's vision, though rich in symbolism, also describes real history and real people, though from a heavenly perspective.

More Than a Woman

John describes the struggles surrounding the birth and mission of the Messiah. He shows, symbolically, the roles that Satan, the Caesars, and the Herods would play. Yet the centerpiece of Revelation 12, the most prominent element, is the woman who is the ark of the covenant.

If she is more than an embodied idea, who is she?

Tradition tells us that she is the same person whom Jesus calls "woman" in John's gospel, the reprise of the person Adam calls "woman" in the garden of Eden. Like the beginning of John's gospel, this episode of the Apocalypse repeatedly evokes the *Protoevangelium* of Genesis. The first clue is that John—here, as in the gospel—never reveals this person's name; he refers to her only by the name Adam gave to Eve in the garden: she is "woman." Later in the same chapter of the Apocalypse, we learn also that, like Eve—who was "mother of all the living" (Gen 3:20)—the woman of John's vision is mother not only to the "male child" but also to "the rest of her offspring," further identified as "those who keep the commandments of God and bear testimony to Jesus" (Rev 12:17). Her offspring, then, are all those who have new life in Jesus Christ. The New Eve, then, fulfills the promise of the old to be, more perfectly, the mother of all the living.

Revelation's most explicit reference to the *Protoevangelium,* however, is the figure of the dragon, whom John clearly identifies with the "ancient serpent" of Genesis, "the deceiver of the world" (Rev 12:9; see

Gen 3:13). The conflict that follows, then, between the dragon and the child clearly fulfills the promise of Genesis 3:15, when God swore to place "enmity" between the serpent "and the woman; between your seed and her seed." And the anguish of the woman's delivery seems also to come in fulfillment of God's words to Eve: "I will greatly multiply your pain in childbearing; in pain you shall bring forth children" (Gen 3:16).

John clearly intends for the woman of the Apocalypse to evoke Eve, the mother of all the living, and the New Eve, the person he identifies as "woman" in the gospel.

Mary, Mary, Reliquary?

We are left with the question, however, of how this woman can also be the revered ark of the covenant.

To understand this, we must first consider what made the ark so holy. It wasn't the acacia wood or the gold ornaments. Nor was it the carved figures of angels. What made the ark holy was that it contained the covenant. Inside that golden box were the ten commandments, the Word of God inscribed by the finger of God; the manna, the miracle bread sent by God to feed His people in the wilderness; and the priestly rod of Aaron.

Whatever made the ark holy made Mary even holier. If the first ark contained the Word of God in stone,

Mary's body contained the Word of God enfleshed. If the first ark contained miraculous bread from heaven, Mary's body contained the very Bread of Life that conquers death forever. If the first ark contained the rod of the long-ago ancestral priest, Mary's body contained the divine person of the eternal priest, Jesus Christ.

What John saw in the heavenly temple was far greater than the ark of the old covenant—the ark that had radiated the glory cloud before the menorah, at the heart of the temple of ancient Israel. John saw the ark of the *new* covenant, the vessel chosen to bear God's covenant into the world once and for all.

Objections Overruled?

The Fathers of the early Church gave strong testimony to this identification of Mary with the ark of the covenant. Still, some interpreters raised objections, which the Fathers answered in turn.

Some objected, for example, because the woman's birth pangs seemed to contradict the long-standing tradition that Mary suffered no pain in labor. Many Christians believe that, since Mary was conceived without original sin, she was exempt from the curses of Genesis 3:16; thus, she would feel no anguish in childbirth.

Yet the anguish of the woman does not necessarily

stand for physical labor pains. Elsewhere in the New Testament, Saint Paul uses the pain of childbirth as a metaphor for spiritual suffering, for suffering in general, or for the longing of the world as it waits for ultimate fulfillment (Gal 4:19; Rom 8:22). The anguish of the woman of the Apocalypse could represent the desire to bring Christ to the world; or it could represent the spiritual sufferings that were the price of Mary's motherhood.

Other interpreters worried that mention of the woman's "other offspring" contradicted the dogma of Mary's perpetual virginity. After all, how could she bear other children if she remained forever a virgin? (We will discuss this matter in greater detail in Chapter 5.) But again, these offspring need not be her physical children. The apostles often speak of themselves as "fathers" to the first generation of Christians (see 1 Cor 4:15). The "other offspring" of Revelation 12 are surely those "who bear testimony to Jesus," and so become His brothers, sharing His Father in heaven—and His mother.

Still other interpreters are simply mystified by the details of John's account—for example, when the woman was "given the two wings of the great eagle that she might fly from the serpent into the wilderness" (Rev 12:14). Such passages are open to a variety of interpretations. Some commentators believe that this depicts

Mary's divine protection from sin and from diabolical influence. Some, too, have seen it as a stylized narrative of the flight into Egypt (Mt 2:13–15), where the Holy Family was driven by the Herodian beast.

Heading for the Hills

The greatest difficulty for interpreters, however, seems to be the apparent uniqueness of John's typological insight in Revelation. Where else, after all, is Mary called the ark of the covenant? Yet closer study of the New Testament shows us that John's insight was not unique—more explicit than others, certainly, but not unique.

Along with John's books, the writings of Luke are the Bible's other great gold mine of Marian doctrine. It is Luke who tells the story of the angel's annunciation to Mary, of Mary's visitation to Elizabeth, of the miraculous circumstances of Jesus' birth, of the Virgin's purification in the temple, of her search for her Son at age twelve, and of her presence among the apostles at the first Pentecost.

Luke was a meticulous literary artist who could claim the additional benefit of having the Holy Spirit as his coauthor. Down through the centuries, scholars have marveled at the way Luke's gospel subtly parallels key texts of the Old Testament. One of the early examples in his narrative is the story of Mary's visitation to Elizabeth.

Luke's language seems to echo the account, in the second book of Samuel, of David's travels as he brought the ark of the covenant to Jerusalem. The story begins as David "arose and went" (2 Sam 6:2). Luke's account of the visitation begins with the same words: Mary "arose and went" (1:39). In their journeys, then, both Mary and David proceeded to the hill country of Judah. David acknowledges his unworthiness with the words "How can the ark of the Lord come to me?" (2 Sam 6:9)—words we find echoed as Mary approaches her kinswoman Elizabeth: "Why is this granted me, that the mother of my Lord should come to me?" (Lk 1:43). Note here that the sentence is almost verbatim, except that "ark" is replaced by "mother." We read further that David "danced" for joy in the presence of the ark (2 Sam 6:14,16), and we find a similar expression used to describe the leaping of the child within Elizabeth's womb as Mary approached (Lk 1:44). Finally, the ark remained in the hill country for three months (2 Sam 6:11), the same amount of time Mary spent with Elizabeth (Lk 1:56).

Why, though, would Luke be so coy about this? Why not just come right out and call the Blessed Virgin a fulfillment of the type of the ark?

Cardinal Newman addressed this question in an interesting manner: "It is sometimes asked, Why do not the sacred writers mention our Lady's greatness? I answer, she was, or may have been alive, when the apostles and evangelists wrote; there was just one book of Scripture certainly written after her death and that book [the book of Revelation] does (so to say) canonize and crown her."

Was Luke, in his quiet way, showing Mary to be the ark of the new covenant? The evidence is too strong to explain credibly in any other way.

Primary Cullers

The woman of the Apocalypse is the ark of the covenant in the heavenly temple; and that woman is the Virgin Mary. This does not, however, preclude other readings of Revelation 12. Scripture, after all, is not a code to be cracked, but a mystery we could never plumb in a lifetime.

In the fourth century, for example, Saint Ambrose saw the woman clearly as the Virgin Mary, "because she is mother of the Church, for she brought forth Him who is the Head of the Church"; yet Ambrose also saw Revelation's woman as an allegory of the Church herself. Saint Ephrem of Syria reached the same conclusion, fearing no contradiction: "The Virgin Mary is, again, the figure of the Church. . . . Let us call the Church by the name of Mary; for she is worthy of the double name."

Saint Augustine, too, held that the woman of the Apocalypse "signifies Mary, who, being spotless, brought forth our spotless Head. Who herself also showed forth in herself a figure of holy Church, so that as she in bringing forth a Son remained a virgin, so the Church also should during the whole of time be bringing forth His members, and yet not lose her virgin estate."

As Mary birthed Christ to the world, so the Church births believers, "other Christs," to each generation. As the Church becomes mother to believers in baptism, so Mary becomes mother to believers as brothers of Christ. The Church, in the words of one recent scholar, "reproduces the mystery of Mary."

We can read all of these interpretations as a gloss on a striking passage of Irenaeus, which we encountered in the last chapter. For the male child is, without doubt, "the pure one opening purely that pure womb which regenerates men unto God." And the "other offspring" we see in Revelation are just as surely those who are regenerated unto God, those who are born of the same womb as Jesus Christ.

Read in the light of the fathers, Revelation 12 can illumine our subsequent reading of all the New Testament passages that describe Christians as brothers of Christ. The Greek word for "brother," *adelphos,* literally means "from the same womb." From John and Irenaeus through Ephrem and Augustine, the early Christians believed that womb belonged to Mary.

The passage proves to be remarkably rich. Other Fathers saw the woman of the Apocalypse as a symbol of Israel, which gave birth to the Messiah; or as the people of God through all the ages; or as the Davidic empire, set in contrast to the Herodians and the Caesars.

She is all these things, even as she is the ark of the covenant. Yet while each of these interpretations suffices in a subsidiary or secondary way, none can fulfill the primary meaning of the text. All of these symbolic readings point beyond themselves to a primary meaning that is literal-historical. Or as Cardinal Newman put it: "The holy apostle would not have spoken of the Church under this particular image unless there had existed a Blessed Virgin Mary who was exalted on high and the object of veneration of all the faithful."

The woman of the Apocalypse must, in the words of another scholar, be "a concrete person who embodies a collective." The primary meaning, moreover—for the woman as for her male child—must belong to the individual, the historical person, the Blessed Virgin Mary, who at once became mother to Christ and the members of His body, the Church.

CHAPTER 4

Power Behind the Throne

The Queen Mother and the Davidic King

We've seen, in both John's gospel and the book of Revelation, how the redemptive work of Jesus fulfills many types, or foreshadowings, in the book of Genesis. The primal creation foreshadowed the renewal and redemption of creation by Jesus Christ (Rev 21:5). The garden of Eden was a type of the garden of Gethsemane. The tree in Eden foreshadowed the wood of the cross. Adam was a type of Jesus Christ; Eve was a type of the Blessed Virgin Mary.

In examining Revelation 12, however, we also glimpsed other patterns of typology. One pattern—considering Mary as the ark of the covenant—inevitably leads us back to Moses, who sojourned with Israel in the desert for forty years. Following Moses, Israel "conquered . . . by the blood of the Lamb" (Rev 12:11) when they ransomed their firstborn at the first Passover. In the same way, the new Israel "conquered . . . by the blood of the Lamb," Jesus Christ, who is the new Moses, the new lawgiver. Following this pattern, we can also see that Moses' sister, whose name was Miriam (Mary), was, like Eve, a failed matriarch, giving in to idolatry and rebellion against God's appointed authority. In the new covenant, however, a new Miriam would fulfill the type and model perfect obedience.

Still, perhaps a more striking pattern of typology is to be found in the kingdom of David. It was David's kingdom that gave ancient Israel its vision of the kingdom of the Messiah. The second Hebrew king, David unified the twelve tribes and established Jerusalem as the nation's capital and spiritual center. The people revered David for his righteousness, justice, and faithfulness to the Lord. David's successors, however, never quite lived up to their forefather's virtue. Whereas David unified the nation, later kings instilled resentment among the tribes. Resentment eventually led to revolt and the dissolution of the unified kingdom of Israel. Weakened Israel was then more vulnerable to its foreign enemies. In time the land was overrun by Babylonian invaders, its people taken into captivity, and David's line completely wiped out—or almost completely. Zedekiah, the last Davidic king, was made to watch while the Chaldeans, his enemies, executed all his sons; they then gouged out Zedekiah's eyes so that the last image etched in his memory would be the corpses of his sons—and the apparent end of the Davidic dynasty (see 2 Kgs 25:7).

Yet through exile and all the ups and downs of their subsequent history, the people of Israel would look back to the kingdom of David as an ideal—and look forward to its future completion with the coming of the Messiah, God's anointed priest-king. Even in Jesus' day, the Pharisees did not hesitate to identify the Messiah as "the Son of David" (Mt 22:42). For the Lord had promised David that a king in his line would one day rule all the nations, and he would reign forever: "I will raise up your offspring after you, who shall come forth from your body. . . . And I will establish the throne of his kingdom forever. I will be his father, and he shall be My son" (2 Sam 7:12–14). We find the promise cited in the Psalms as well: "The Lord swore to David a sure oath from which He will not turn back: 'One of the sons of your body I will set on your throne. . . . Their sons also forever shall sit upon your throne.' For the Lord has chosen Zion for his habitation: 'This is My dwelling place forever' " (Ps 132:11–13).

The prophets expressed Israel's combination of nostalgia and longing, and they foretold the Messiah's coming with amazing accuracy. Even before the time of Zedekiah, Isaiah foretold that David's line—the family tree of David's father, Jesse—would be reduced to a "stump," but from that stump would come forth "a shoot," "a branch": the Messiah (Is 11:1). "Hear then, O house of David! . . . The Lord Himself will give you a sign. Behold, a virgin shall conceive and bear a son, and shall call his name Immanuel" (Is 7:13–14).

I Dream of Genealogy

The very first words of the New Testament fulfill the promise of the prophets and the longing of Israel: "The book of the genealogy of Jesus Christ, the son of David" (Mt 1:1). From the beginning Matthew identifies Jesus as the son of David, the long-awaited Messiah. Yet he does this in an odd, almost unprecedented, way. Though a genealogy was traditionally a chronicle of male succession, Matthew anomalously incorporates the names of four women. These women, moreover, all fall far from Israel's ideal of purity—moral or racial.

The first mentioned is Tamar (Mt 1:3), a Canaanite woman who had sexual relations with her father-in-law (Gen 38:15–18). The second is Rahab, a prostitute and a pagan Canaanite (Mt 1:5; Jos 2:1–24). The third is Ruth, another pagan, a Moabite (Mt 1:5). And the last, significantly, is Bathsheba, "the wife of Uriah" the Hittite (Mt 1:6); it is Bathsheba, of course, who committed adultery with King David.

Matthew seems to flout the rules by listing women in Jesus' genealogy; but he is actually doing something clever: a preemptive apologetic strike. By placing women—*pagan* women, and pagan women of shady reputation—among Jesus' ancestors, Matthew effectively undercuts the arguments of anyone who would question Jesus' messianic credentials. For surely the evangelist knew that the claim of Jesus' virginal conception would evoke wry smiles from skeptics. (And it certainly did. Jesus is called a bastard in several places in the Talmud, and the title "Son of Mary" itself was probably a slur. The Jewish custom was to call a man "son of" his father. Only a fatherless man would be called "son of" his mother.) Yet Matthew almost dares his fellow Jewish readers to raise questions about Jesus' ancestry. Because if Jews derided Jesus as "son of Mary," then King Solomon, *the prototypical son of David*, would lose four times over. For Solomon shared those same female ancestors with Jesus—and the last of them, Bathsheba, was Solomon's own mother.

Matthew is safeguarding Jesus' messianic credentials at the same time he's showing the divine handiwork in the virginal conception. Without the Davidic matrix—the kingdom, the promise, and the prophecies—no one can truly understand the coming of Christ. The evangelist continues this oblique line of argument by quoting Isaiah's prediction about the virginal conception of Immanuel, "God with us" (Mt 1:23). A few lines later, when Matthew recounts Jesus' birth in Bethlehem, the city of David, he cites Micah 5:2: "And you, O Bethlehem . . . from you shall come a ruler who will govern my people Israel" (Mt 2:6). Finally, concluding his infancy narrative, Matthew depicts the Holy Family settling "in a city called Nazareth" (2:23). The root of the word "Nazareth" is *netser,* or "branch"—and "branch" was the name that Isaiah gave to the Messiah, who would spring up one day from the stump of Jesse's tree (Is 11:1).

Seeing Stars

Thus, from the beginning of the New Testament, we see that the Davidic kingdom, like the garden of Eden, was a singular anticipation of the coming of Jesus Christ. In this light, the small details of David's monarchy—again like the small details of the *Protoevangelium*—take on enormous significance. The structure of David's monarchy was neither incidental nor accidental; in God's providential plan, it foreshadowed the kingdom of God.

At the end of the New Testament, in the book of Revelation, the Davidic typology continues as chapters 11 and 12 invoke Psalm 2, the psalm of the Davidic king. The psalm begins, "Why do the nations rage, and the people plot in vain?" Revelation, in turn, shows how "the nations raged," bringing upon themselves God's "wrath" (Rev 11:18; see also Ps 2:5). In Psalm 2, God tells the Davidic king: "You are My son, today I have begotten you" (v. 7)—anticipating the words spoken to Jesus at His baptism: "This is My beloved son, with whom I am well pleased" (Mt 3:17). The son of David would rule "the nations" with a "rod of iron," according to Psalm 2:8–9. In Revelation, this promise is fulfilled as "the woman" brings forth her "male child," who will "rule all the nations with a rod of iron" (Rev 12:5).

Continuing our study of Revelation, then, in light of Davidic typology, how should we understand the "woman," this royal figure "clothed with the sun" and crowned with the stars?

First, it is clear that this woman must hold an exalted place in relation to Israel, whose twelve tribes are represented by the twelve stars that crown her head. Indeed, John's vision evokes the dream of the patriarch Joseph in the book of Genesis, of "the sun, the moon, and eleven stars . . . bowing down" to him (37:9). In Joseph's dream, the eleven stars stand for his brothers, his fellow tribal patriarchs.

Yet there's still more to Revelation's woman. For in the most glorious days of the old covenant, the twelve tribes would indeed be united, and would pay obeisance to a female royal figure; and this figure surely foreshadows the woman we meet in the Apocalypse.

The Queen Mother

Israel's monarchy arose in very specific historic circumstances in a particular geographic region. In the ancient Near East, most nations were monarchies ruled by a king. In addition, most cultures practiced polygamy; so a given king often had several wives. This posed problems. First, whom should the people honor as queen? But more important, whose son should receive the right of succession to the throne?

In most Near Eastern cultures, these twin problems were resolved by a single custom. The woman ordinarily honored as queen was not the wife of the king, but the mother of the king. There was an element of justice to the practice, since it was often the persuasive (or seductive) power of the mother that won the throne for her son. The custom also served as a stabilizing factor in national cultures. As wife of the former king and mother to the present king, the queen mother embodied the continuity of dynastic succession.

The office of the queen mother was well established among the gentiles by the time the people of Israel began to clamor for a monarchy. For Israel had not always been a kingdom. In God's plan, *God* was to be their king (1 Sam 8:7). But the people begged the prophet Samuel to give them a king: "We will have a king over us, that we also may be like all the nations" (1 Sam 8:19–20). God, then, allowed the people to have their way. But for His glory: Israel's monarchy would providentially foreshadow the kingship of God's own Son. Israel's kingdom would be a type of the kingdom of God.

Historically, this played out as the people looked around them for models of governance. Remember, they wanted a king in order to be "like all the nations." Thus, following the models of the neighboring lands, they established a dynasty, a legal system, a royal court—and a queen mother. We find this in Israel at the beginning of the Davidic dynasty. David's first successor, Solomon, reigns with his mother, Bathsheba, at his right hand. Israel's queen mother, or *gebirah* ("great lady"), appears, then, throughout the history of the monarchy, to the very end. When Jerusalem falls to Babylon, we find the invaders taking away the king, Jehoiachin, and also his mother, Nehushta, who is given precedence, in the account, over the king's wives (2 Kgs 24:15; see also Jer 13:18).

Between Bathsheba and Nehushta there were many queen mothers. Some worked for good, some didn't; but none was a mere figurehead. *Gebirah* was more than a title; it was an office with real authority. Consider the following scene from early in Solomon's reign: "So Bathsheba went to King Solomon, to speak to him on behalf of Adonijah. And the king rose to meet her, and bowed down to her; then he sat on his throne, and had a seat brought for the king's mother; and she sat on his right" (1 Kgs 2:19).

This short passage packs implicit volumes about Israel's court protocol and power structure. First, we see that the queen mother was approaching her son in order to speak on behalf of another person. This confirms what we know about queen mothers in other Near Eastern cultures. We see in the epic of Gilgamesh, for example, that the queen mother in Mesopotamia was considered an intercessor, or advocate, for the people.

Next, we notice that Solomon rose from his throne when his mother entered the room. This makes the queen mother unique among the royal subjects. Anyone else would, following protocol, rise in Solomon's presence; even the king's wives were required to bow before him (1 Kgs 1:16). Yet Solomon rose to honor Bathsheba. Moreover, he showed further respect by bowing before her and by seating her in the place of greatest honor, at his right hand. Undoubtedly, this describes a court ritual of Solomon's time; but all ritual expresses real relationships. What do Solomon's actions tell us about his status in relation to his mother?

First, his power and authority are in no way threatened by her. He bows to her, but *he* remains the monarch. She sits at his right hand, not vice versa.

Yet clearly he will honor her requests—not out of any legally binding obligation of obedience, but rather out of filial love. By the time of this particular scene, Solomon clearly had a track record of granting his mother's wishes. When Adonijah first approaches Bathsheba to beg her intercession, he says, "Pray ask King Solomon—*he will not refuse you*." Though technically Solomon was Bathsheba's superior, in the orders of both nature and protocol he remained her son.

He relied on her, too, to be his chief counselor, who could advise and instruct him in a way, perhaps, that few subjects would have the courage to follow. Chapter 31 of the book of Proverbs provides a striking illustration of how seriously a king took the queen mother's counsel.

Introduced as "the words of Lemuel, king of Massa, which his mother taught him," the chapter goes on to give substantial, practical instruction in governance. We're not talking about folk wisdom here. As a political adviser and even strategist, as an advocate for the people, and as a subject who could be counted on for frankness, the queen mother was unique in her relationship to the king.

The Key of David

Without the Davidic matrix we cannot begin to understand the coming of Jesus Christ. For His Davidic ancestry was essential not only to His self-understanding but also to the expectations of His contemporaries, and to the theological reflection of His first followers, such as Saint Paul and Saint John. The Messiah would be David's son, yet also God's son (see 2 Sam 7:12–14). The everlasting king would come from David's house, from David's "body." When the "male child" came to rule the nations, He would rule as a Davidic king, with a rod of iron, as David himself had sung.

Yet this typological relationship would not cease with the fact of kingship; it would include many of the small details of the monarchy. As David established a holy city in Jerusalem, so his ultimate successor would create a heavenly Jerusalem. As David's first successor reigned beside his queen mother, so would David's final and everlasting successor. The Davidic monarchy finds its perfect fulfillment in the reign of Jesus Christ—and there was *never* a Davidic king without a Davidic queen: the king's own mother, the queen mother.

Only with this Davidic key can we unlock the mysteries, for example, of the wedding feast at Cana. Mary approaches her son to intercede for the people—just as Bathsheba spoke to Solomon on behalf of Adonijah. Mary counsels her son about the matter at hand; yet she counsels others to obey *Him* and not her. Jesus, then, speaks to His mother as her superior; yet He defers to her suggestion—just as one might expect a Davidic king to grant the wish of his queen mother.

This same key of David also unlocks the mysteries of the "woman" of the book of Revelation. She is crowned with twelve stars—representing the twelve tribes of Israel—because she will bear the Davidic king. She is threatened by the dragon because the serpent's allies, the house of Herod, would set themselves against the reign of David's house and David's successor.

Finally, the Davidic monarchy completes the connection between the original Adam and Eve, who failed, and the New Adam and New Eve, who succeeded and won redemption for the human race.

In Genesis we see that Adam was created first and was given dominion, or kingship, over the earth. Yet he was never intended to reign by himself: "The Lord God said, 'It is not good that the man should be alone' " (Gen 2:18). So God created Eve, Adam's helpmate and queen. They are to share dominion. When Adam awoke to find her, he said, "This at last is bone of my bones and flesh of my flesh" (Gen 2:23), a phrase that, significantly, appears elsewhere in the Bible—when the tribes of Israel declare David their king. In acclaiming the youth, they say: "We are your bone and flesh" (2 Sam 5:1). Thus, Adam's words take on greater significance: they are a royal acclamation.

In Genesis, after Adam exults, the author comments: "Therefore a man leaves his father and his mother and cleaves to his wife" (Gen 2:24). Ancient commentators puzzled over this text, for many reasons. One was that, in the ancient cultures, it was the woman who left her family at marriage; yet here it is "a man." Most puzzling, however, is Genesis's reference to father and mother in this context, since Adam had no father or mother. In citing this text from Genesis, Saint Paul acknowledges that this is a profound mystery, but he solves the mystery in the same breath: "I am saying that it refers to Christ and the Church" (Eph 5:32). It is Jesus Who would leave

Father and mother to be united to His bride, the Church.

Creation's initial monarchy would not achieve God's purpose—nor would the Davidic monarchy—but something later would. A New Adam—Jesus—would reign, as had been foreshadowed in the garden and in the courts of Solomon. The New Adam, the new Davidic monarch, would reign with His bride, the New Eve, and she would be a real historical woman, whom Revelation would identify with the Church. She would be mother of the living. She would be advocate of the people. She would be queen mother. She would be Mary.

CHAPTER 5

From Typing to Teaching

The Mother Is the Message

THE STUDY OF biblical typology can easily consume an avid reader—or an amateur detective. It's fascinating to search out the ways in which, as Saint Augustine said, the New Testament is concealed in the Old, and the Old is revealed in the New. Typology uncovers a hidden dimension to every page of the scriptures; careful study shows us that God writes history the way men write words, and that He is an author of supremely subtle artistry and meticulous craft. He wastes no words in revelation; nothing is incidental or accidental in God's providence.

Typology is liberating. It frees us from the slavish reading of biblical texts in isolation from all other biblical texts and in isolation from Tradition. Typology can also be illuminating, revealing the richness of passages that had formerly seemed obscure or trivial.

Yet typology has its own pitfalls, and its abuses have led some scholars far afield and others into heresy. To avoid these excesses, it's important that we be clear about our purposes, that we begin with an end in mind. When we read scripture in a typological way, we're not trying to crack a code, or solve a puzzle, or impose our own fanciful visions on the inspired word. We're trying to encounter a person. We want to know God, His ways, His plan, His chosen people—and His mother.

Thus we want to avoid a danger I call atomism—concentrating on biblical types in isolation, as if they were disconnected metaphors or individual specimens in a laboratory dish. Nor are we talking about some occult system of symbols when we consider the typology of Eve, the ark of the covenant, and the queen mother. We're looking at creatures ordained by providence to come to fulfillment in a real, historical person. Just as Isaac, Moses, and David were real people who foreshadowed the divine Messiah, Jesus, so Eve, and the ark, and the queen mother give us glimpses of the great reality that is Mary.

She, then, must be our goal as we study her types. For she was and she remains a real, living person; and a person is an irreducible mystery, not the sum of his or her symbols. Paul was moved by the way Jesus was foreshadowed in Adam; but Paul was in love with Jesus Christ. So we must come to know and love *Mary herself* as she is illuminated by her biblical types.

This is not something optional for Christians. It is not something ornamental in the gospel. Mary is—in a real, abiding, and spiritual sense—our mother. If we are to know the brotherhood of Jesus Christ, we must come to know the mother whom we share with Jesus Christ. Without her, our understanding of the gospel will be, at best, partial. Without her, our understanding of salvation can never be familial. It will be stalled out in the old covenant, where God's fatherhood was considered to be metaphorical, and man's sonship was more like servility.

Who is this woman, then—this mother, this chosen vessel of God and of all believers? She is a historical person, and the Church has carefully preserved certain historical facts about her in the scriptural accounts and in the form of dogmas.

Keeping the Faith

What is dogma? A useful definition comes from Cardinal Joseph Ratzinger, who wrote that "dogma is by definition nothing other than an interpretation of Scripture."

The cardinal's insight was confirmed by the Church's International Theological Commission in its 1989 document *On the Interpretation of Dogmas:* "In the dogma of the Church, one is thus concerned with the correct interpretation of the Scriptures." Dogma, then, is the Church's infallible exegesis of scripture.

There are certain facts of Mary's life that the Bible teaches explicitly. Her virginal conception of Jesus, for example, is put forth clearly and unequivocally in Luke's gospel (1:34–35). Other facts are *implicit* in the biblical text, but have always been taught by the Church, such as Mary's assumption into heaven and her immaculate conception. The truth of these implicit facts is no less important for our understanding of the gospel. In fact, implicit details are often *more important* to a narrative, because they show us what the narrator takes for granted. Though these details—assumptions, if you will—remain unspoken, they make up the fabric in which the narrative is woven. Without their tacit presence, the narrative disintegrates.

Thus, down through the centuries, the Church has carefully preserved, protected, and defended its Marian teachings, because to give them up would be to give up the gospel. To suppress them would be to deprive God's family of its mother. Without the dogmas, Mary becomes unreal: a random female body from Nazareth, insignificant in her individuality, incidental to the gospels' narrative. And when Mary becomes unreal, so does the incarnation of God, which depended upon Mary's consent; so does the suffering flesh of Christ, which He took from His mother; so does the Christian's status as a child of God, which depends upon our sharing in the household and family of Jesus, the Son of David, the Son of Mary.

Together with the scriptural accounts, the Church's Marian dogmas keep us close to the incarnate reality of God's family. Again, for a believing Christian, neither the dogmas nor the types should be abstractions or metaphors. They are aspects of a living person, our mother.

Consider the Christian example of Saint John of Damascus, a Father of the Church who loved the scriptures so much that he moved to Jerusalem in order to live within their landscape. He knew, in a profound way, all the Old Testament types of Mary and Jesus. And he knew the facts of Mary's life, including those that had not yet been officially declared as dogmas. Around 740 A.D., he preached three homilies on Mary's assumption into heaven, and he incorporated many of the dogmas of the Church and the types we've discussed in this book: the new Eve, the ark of the covenant, the queen mother. Yet all the while, John never preached about ideas; he interpreted the scriptures as he preached about a person, a person who had been taken by God to heaven.

His evocation of Mary's reception into heaven is especially telling. "David her forefather, and her father in God, dances with joy," he said, "and the angels dance with him, and the archangels applaud." In imagining this scene, John did not see King David dancing around a dogma, or around a metaphor for the ark of the covenant (2 Sam 6:14). Rather, John saw David dancing out of love for a person, who was his daughter and yet his mother.

It is, however, dogma—the Church's infallible interpretation of scripture—that enables us to see this real mother as clearly as David did. For the dogmas are facts of faith that preserve a certain vision of God's family.

God's Plan of Salvation: Immaculately Conceived

The immaculate conception is the doctrine that God preserved Mary free from all stain of original sin. From the first moment of her conception in the womb of her mother, then, she lived in a state of sanctifying grace won for her by the merits of her son, Jesus. Thus the angel's greeting to Mary, "Hail, full of grace," was uttered years before Jesus won grace for mankind. Yet Mary was, even then, "full of grace."

Cardinal John Henry Newman taught that the immaculate conception was an important corollary to Mary's role as the New Eve. He asked: "If Eve was raised above human nature by that indwelling moral gift which we call grace, is it rash to say that Mary had even a greater grace? . . . And if Eve had this supernatural inward gift given her from the first moment of her personal existence, is it possible to deny that Mary too had this gift from the very first moment of her personal existence?"

Newman also found it fitting for Christ to be born of a sinless mother.

> *Mary was no mere instrument in God's dispensation. The Word of God . . . did not merely pass through her, as He may pass through us in Holy Communion. It was no heavenly body which the Eternal Son assumed. . . . No, He imbibed, He sucked up her blood and her substance into His Divine Person. He became man from her, and received her lineaments and her features as the appearance and character under which He should manifest Himself to*

the world. He was known, doubtless, by His likeness to her, to be her Son. . . . Was it not fitting . . . that the Eternal Father should prepare her for this ministration by some preeminent sanctification?

The immaculate conception was a commonplace of the early Church. Saint Ephrem of Syria testified to it in the fourth century, as did Saint Augustine in the fifth. Augustine put the doctrine in its proper, familial context, saying that it would be an offense against Jesus to say that His mother was a sinner. All have sinned, said Augustine, "except the holy Virgin Mary, concerning whom, for the honor of the Lord, I wish no question to be raised at all, when we are treating of sins. After all, how do we know what greater degree of grace for a complete victory over sin was conferred on her who merited to conceive and bring forth Him Who all admit was without sin."

While in the West theologians have taught the doctrine somewhat negatively, emphasizing Mary's sinlessness, the Eastern churches have always put the accent, instead, on her abundant holiness. The affectionate colloquial term for her is *Panagia,* the All-Holy; for everything in her is holy.

Still, the Church did not make a dogmatic pronouncement on the immaculate conception until 1854. In the meantime, some Christians—even some saints—worried that to say that Mary's sinlessness proceeded from the moment of her conception would somehow nullify her human nature or Christ's saving work. Yet Pope Pius IX addressed these concerns completely as he solemnly defined the dogma "that the most Blessed Virgin Mary, in the first instant of her conception, by a singular grace and privilege granted by Almighty God, in view of the merits of Jesus Christ, the Savior of the human race, was preserved free from all stain of Original Sin."

That's less than a single sentence, but it's densely packed with teaching. Pope Pius makes it clear that the immaculate conception is a unique ("singular") grace of God, just as the incarnation of Jesus is a unique event in history. Next, he states unequivocally that this singular grace was won for Mary by Jesus Christ, her Savior. And finally, the pope emphasizes that the immaculate conception is a divine act of preservation—a work of God, and not a work of Mary herself.

The immaculate conception, then, was a fruit of the redemption applied to Mary by way of anticipation; for the redemption was always in view for the eternal God, Who is not bound by time as we are. Thus, Christ's redemption applies to you and me, though we could not be there at Calvary—and it applied to Mary at the moment of her creation, though Christ's saving death was still years away. Her redemption was an act of preservation, while for all others it is an act of deliverance.

Even today, we can see that Christ, in an analogous way, rescues some sinners by deliverance and others by preservation. Some people turn away from sinful habits, such as shoplifting, drug abuse, or adultery, after they receive the grace of conversion. But others reject sin habitually from an early age because God has given them the grace of a good upbringing in a Christian family. Either way, by preservation or deliverance, redemption is a work of God. In His providential plan, He found it fitting that Mary should be preserved from sin completely, all the days of her life.

If Mary was sinless, did she really need Jesus to redeem her? Yes, she did. Her singular preservation could not have taken place without the redemption won for all men by Jesus. Jesus is God, and so He is both our creator and our redeemer. In the very act of creating Mary, he redeemed her from any limitations of human nature or susceptibility to sin. She is a creature, but she is His mother, and He has perfectly fulfilled the commandment to honor her. He honored her in a way that is singularly beautiful.

Fetal Attraction

As we pray the Hail Mary, we echo one of the most ancient titles Christians have given to Mary: Mother of God (in Greek, *Theotokos,* literally "God-bearer"). As early as the third century (and probably earlier), the Church in Egypt prayed: "We fly to your patronage, O holy Mother of God . . ." Early Fathers such as Saint Clement of Alexandria, Origen, and Saint Alexander called upon Mary as "Mother of God" or its equivalent, "Mother of the Lord." This prayer of Christians follows Elizabeth's inspired greeting of Mary, her kinswoman: "And why is this granted me, that the mother of my Lord should come to me?" (Lk 1:43).

With such scriptural precedent, the title "Mother of God" went uncontested in the first centuries of the Church. Moreover, the statement follows logically from a Christian's necessary acknowledgment of Christ's divinity. If He is God and Mary is His mother, then she is the Mother of God.

The traditional use of "Mother of God" depended upon a theological principle called the *communication of idioms.* According to this principle, whatever one says about either of Christ's natures can be said truly of Christ Himself; for the two natures, divine and human, were united in Him, in one person. Thus, for example, Christians can boldly say that God the Son died on the cross at Calvary, even though God is surely immortal. Thus, too, Christians have always maintained that God was born in a manger in Bethlehem, even though God is surely eternal.

In the fifth century, however, some theologians began to raise scruples about the title "Mother of God," worrying that it implied Mary was somehow the "originator" of God. They could accept the title "Mother of Christ," they said, but not "Mother of God." They further argued against the unity of Christ's natures, saying that the Virgin gave birth to Christ's *human* nature but not His *divine* nature.

The Church disagreed, and Mary's title was vigorously defended by Pope Celestine I, who drew strong support from Saint Cyril of Alexandria, a leading theologian of the day. Cyril pointed out that a mother does not give birth to a nature; she gives birth to a person. Mary gave birth to Jesus Christ, Who was and is a divine person. Though Mary did not originate God, she most certainly bore Him. She "mothered" Him.

To us, the dispute might seem abstract and academic, but its progress consumed the attention even of ordinary Christians in the fifth century, stirring them to more fervent devotion. History tells us that when Pope Celestine convoked the Council of Ephesus (A.D. 431) in order to settle the "Mother of God" controversy, Christians thronged the city, awaiting word of the bishops' decision. When the bishops read the council's proclamation that Mary was indeed the Mother of God, the people gave way to their joy and celebrated by carrying the bishops (all two hundred of them!) aloft through the streets in a torchlit procession.

Think, for a moment, about the intensity of the affection those believers felt for the Blessed Virgin Mary—to sojourn to the city of the council, to wait outdoors for the bishops' decree, then to spend the night in celebration, all because this woman had received her due honor. They would not act this way out of love for an academic argument. Nor would they celebrate the triumph of a metaphor. I daresay they would not make the perilous journey to Ephesus for the sake of any other mother: only for their own. For their own mother was also the Mother of God.

When we call Mary "Mother of God," we share that long-ago joy. For bound up in that phrase is the astonishing fact that we are children of God. We are brothers and sisters of Mary's Son—the God-man—and not just His human nature!

Once a Virgin, Always a Virgin

The gospels of Matthew and Luke leave no room for doubt that Mary was a virgin at the time she conceived the Son of God (Mt 1:18; Lk 1:34–35; 3:23). Of course, the early Fathers and creeds all uphold the truth of the virginal conception. Why has the Church always insisted that Christians believe in Jesus "born of the Virgin Mary"? Because Mary's virginal motherhood is the guarantor of both Jesus' divinity and His humanity. Saint Thomas Aquinas summed it up: "In order that Christ's body might be shown to be a real body, He was born of a woman. In order that His Godhead might be made clear, He was born of a virgin." As we have seen in previous chapters, Mary's virginity is crucial also to Tradition's understanding of her as the New Eve.

Thus, from the beginning of the Church, Mary's name has almost always appeared with a modifier: "virgin." In the Apostles' Creed, in the Nicene Creed, in the early baptismal creeds of Rome and Africa, believers have consistently professed belief in Jesus "born of the Virgin

Mary." For the first Christians, to believe in Jesus was to believe in Mary's virginity.

Indeed, Mary's identity is incomplete without the word "virgin." She is "the Virgin Mary." Virginity is not merely a characteristic of her personality, or a description of her biological state. Virginity is so much a part of her that it has become like a name. When literature or songs refer to "the Virgin" or "the Blessed Virgin," it can mean only one person: Mary.

"Virgin" is, once and always, who she is. Thus the church has constantly taught that Mary preserved her virginity not only before the conception of Jesus, but ever afterward as well. Though she was married to Joseph, the two never consummated their marriage by sexual intercourse. This doctrine is known as Mary's *perpetual virginity.*

Heretics in the early Church occasionally challenged this teaching, but they never gained much ground. Their purportedly scriptural arguments were easily refuted by the likes of Saint Jerome, the great biblical scholar of the ancient church. (Jerome was also a great name-caller, and he reserved his most scathing insults for those who dared to question Mary's perpetual virginity.) What were the arguments of these heretics?

The bulk of their arguments rested on the New

Testament passages that refer to Jesus' "brethren." We find in Saint Mark's gospel, for example: "Is not this the carpenter, the son of Mary and brother of James and Joses and Judas and Simon, and are not His sisters here with us?" (6:3). In Matthew 12:46, we see: "Behold, His mother and His brethren stood outside, asking to speak to Him." In Luke 2:7, we read that Jesus was Mary's "firstborn."

This is virtually a nonissue for anyone who has a glancing familiarity with Hebrew customs. The Hebrew word for "brother" is a more inclusive term, applying to cousins as well. In fact, in ancient Hebrew there is no word for cousin. To a Jew of Jesus' time, one's cousin was one's brother. This familial principle applied in other Semitic languages as well, such as Aramaic, the language Jesus spoke. Furthermore, precisely *because* Jesus was an only child, His cousins would even assume the legal status of siblings for Him, as they were His nearest relatives. Finally, the word "firstborn" raises no real difficulty, because it was a legal term in ancient Israel that applied to the child who "opened the womb," whether or not the mother bore more children afterward.

Heretics also quoted passages that seemed—again, to those unfamiliar with Jewish modes of expression—to imply that Mary and Joseph later had sexual relations. They would cite Matthew 1:18: "Now the birth of Jesus Christ took place in this way. When His mother Mary had been betrothed to Joseph, before they came together, she was found to be with child of the Holy Spirit." Saint Jerome's antagonist Helvidius placed his question squarely on the word "before" in that sentence, claiming that Matthew would never have applied "before they came together" to a couple who did not eventually come together. Helvidius also cited a passage later in Matthew's first chapter that declares that Joseph "knew her not until she had borne a son" (1:25). Again, Helvidius said that Matthew's use of "until" implied that Joseph "knew" Mary afterward.

This is a classic example of amateur exegesis. It was definitively and easily leveled by a professional biblical scholar. Responding to Helvidius, Jerome demonstrated that scripture "often uses a fixed time . . . to denote time without limitation, as when God by the mouth of the prophet says to certain persons, 'Even to old age I am He' (Is 46:4)." Jerome thundered on: "Will He cease to be God when they have grown old?" The answer, of course, is no. Jerome goes on, then, to quote Jesus, Who said: "Lo, I am with you always, to the close of the age" (Mt 28:20).

Wryly, Jerome asked Helvidius if he thought the Lord would then forsake His disciples *after* the close of the age. Jerome multiplies such examples, but we don't need to repeat them here. Suffice it to say that those who question Mary's virginity don't have a page of scripture to stand on—and Christian Tradition is univocally against them.

If they wanted to find a message implicit in scripture, they should have examined the first chapter of Luke's gospel. There, the angel Gabriel appears to Mary—who was then betrothed to Joseph—and tells her that she will conceive a son. Mary responds: "How shall this be, since I have no husband?" (Lk 1:27–34).

Now, this would be an odd question if Mary had planned to have normal marital relations with her husband. The angel had told her only that she would conceive a son, which is a commonplace event in marriage. If Helvidius were right, then Mary should have known exactly "how shall this be." It would happen in the normal course of nature.

But that, apparently, was beyond the realm of possibility for her. The unspoken assumption behind her question is that, even though she was betrothed, she should not have an opportunity to conceive a child. How can that be? Some commentators speculate that Mary must have vowed virginity from an early age, and that Joseph knew of her vow, accepted it, and eventually took it on himself. Contrarians respond that vowed celibacy was almost unheard of in ancient Israel. Yet we do find examples of celibacy in the time of Jesus, evidenced in the New Testament by Jesus Himself and by Saint Paul, among others. The Dead Sea Scrolls attest that celibacy was a common practice of some Israelite sects. So it is not unthinkable that Mary could have vowed virginity.

In any case, it is clear from scripture and Tradition that she lived her virginity—so much that, for all future generations, she became its very personification. Saint Epiphanius dismissed all arguments against Mary's virginity with the witness of her name. Even in his day (the fourth century), she was well established as simply "the Virgin." A good son firmly defends his mother's honor—though most of the time, he need not do so with long and labored argument. Still, there is a place for proofs as well; and sons of Mary can, if challenged, take up the Scriptures in her defense, as Jerome did.

A Gratuitous Assumption

Earlier we established that Christ honored His mother by preserving her from sin from the first moment of her life.

That would be glory enough, but we know that He didn't stop there. As she received redemption as a first fruit of Christ's work, so she also received bodily resurrection and heavenly glory. We see this in the scripture: "And a great portent appeared in heaven, a woman clothed with the sun, with the moon under her feet, and on her head a crown of twelve stars" (Rev 12:1). Christ brought the ark of the new covenant to dwell in the holy of holies in the temple of the heavenly Jerusalem. This fact we profess as the Assumption of the Blessed Virgin Mary. At the end of her earthly days, Mary was taken up, body and soul, into heaven.

Documentary evidence of the assumption stretches back to the fourth century. By the end of the sixth century, the doctrine and the feast day were already universally established in the Church.

There is no evidence that the teaching was seriously challenged or disputed during the period of the Fathers; nor did any church or city ever claim to own the relics of the Blessed Virgin. That, in itself, is quite remarkable. In the early Church, cities and churches vied with one another for possession of the bones of the great apostles and martyrs. If Mary's bones had remained on earth, they would, of course, have been the grand prize.

The search for her relics and their transfer from city to city would have been well attested. But again, the historical record shows not a hint of a Marian reliquary—aside from her empty tomb. (And two cities claim that prize!)

The most reliable surviving testimonies of the assumption come from the sixth-century Saint Gregory of Tours. Earlier documents, such as the fourth-century *Passing of Mary,* testify to her assumption, but with descriptions that are perhaps too fanciful and extravagant to be believed. We can accept them as testimony to the doctrine without accepting them as authoritative in the small details.

A great theologian and biblical scholar, Saint John of Damascus, left us the most trustworthy and enduring legacy of the assumption. We mentioned earlier that John's three homilies weave together all the biblical types discussed in this book into a single portrait of a mother in heaven. He refers especially to the liturgical readings for the feast and its vigil. They are the same readings the Church uses today.

What do they show us? They show that Christians have always venerated Mary as the Ark of the Covenant. John draws extensively from 1 Chronicles 15, in which

King David assembles all Israel to bring the ark of the Lord to its resting place in Jerusalem. Though John of Damascus never quotes Revelation 11:19–12:17, he repeatedly calls Mary the Ark, and describes David dancing around her upon her arrival in heaven. This connection is continued in the responsorial psalm for the Vigil of the Assumption: "Lord, go up to the place of Your rest, You and the ark of Your holiness" (Ps 132:8). Could a single line more perfectly summarize King David's transfer of the ark—or the Son of David's assumption of the new Ark?

John of Damascus also draws from the typology of Eve and Eden to show that the assumption was a fitting end to Mary's days:

> *This day the Eden of the New Adam welcomes its living Paradise, in whom our sentence has been repealed. . . . Eve gave ear to the message of the serpent . . . and, together with Adam, was condemned to death and assigned to the world of darkness. But how could death swallow this truly blessed soul, who humbly gave ear to the word of God? . . . How could corruption dare touch the body that had contained Life? Such thoughts are abhorrent and totally repugnant in regard to the body and soul of the Mother of God.*

Thus, this last of the Church Fathers makes explicit what was implicit in the doctrine of his second-century predecessors: Mary's status as the New Eve requires our belief in her bodily assumption.

The readings for the feast also show us how the assumption confirms Mary forever as the queen mother. The responsorial psalm of the feast day itself describes the wedding of a Davidic king: "The queen stands at your right hand, arrayed in gold" (Ps 45:9). Yet that line just as surely describes the heavenly court of the ultimate Davidic king, Jesus Christ, who reigns with His queen mother at His right hand—just as Solomon reigned beside Bathsheba. "So it was fitting," said John of Damascus—after calling Christ the New Solomon—"that the Mother should take up her abode in the Royal City of her Son."

Why in heaven would God assume such a queen? She's more than His type. She's His mother. The Damascene gets the last word in that matter: "What honors He has conferred on her—He Who commanded us to honor our parents."

Idol Talk?

Some non-Catholics charge that all these Marian dogmas add up to Mary worship—idolatry pure and simple.

There was a time in my life when I thought so. As a young evangelical, I even passed out tracts identifying Mary with the Babylonian goddess Ishtar, whose worship is described by the prophet Jeremiah (7:18; 44:15–17). Marian devotion, I believed, was nothing more than goddess worship smuggled into Christianity by long-ago pagans who feigned conversion.

I was wrong, of course—first of all, in my belief that Catholics "worship" Mary. In truth, the Church gives her honor and veneration as the greatest of saints, while reserving adoration and worship for God alone. Indeed, the early Christians who were most vigorous in their Marian devotion were equally vigorous in denouncing any local remnants of goddess worship.

I was wrong, too, in condemning the title "queen of heaven" just because it was once applied to a pagan goddess. Anti-Christians use this very argument to discredit the claims of Jesus Christ. Call it the comparative-religions approach. It runs like this: many ancient pagan myths told of a "son of a god" born of a virgin who came to earth, died, and rose from the dead; therefore, the "Jesus myth" is nothing but a late and very successful copycat.

On the contrary! From great Christians like C. S.

Lewis I learned that such parallels between Christianity and paganism are best understood as a preparation for the gospel—God's way of giving even the gentiles a hint (Lewis called these premonitions "strange dreams") of a glorious future that would one day be theirs.

CHAPTER 6

What About the Children?

The Queen Mother and the Royal Family

It can be exhilarating to find out who Mary really is. At the same time, to some people, the facts can be overwhelming—even off-putting. If she is the new ark of the covenant, then like the old ark, she demands our profound reverence. Consider Saint Methodius's prayer to the Blessed Virgin, from the third century:

> *God paid such honor to the ark, which was the image and type of your sanctity, that no one but the priests could approach it open or enter to behold it. The veil separated it off, keeping the vestibule as that of a queen. Then what sort of veneration must we, who are the least of creatures, owe to you who are indeed a queen—to you, the living ark of God, the Lawgiver—to you, the heaven that contains Him Whom none can contain?*

As royalty, Mary can seem remote to those of us who labor at ordinary jobs, who bear no titles of nobility, who hardly distinguish ourselves from the crowd of royal subjects. How can we, dressed in the rags of our sins, approach Mary, who is sinless and enthroned in glory?

To answer that question, we need to recognize the serious spiritual and theological problem that lies behind it. It's not so much a bad Marian image; she *is,* after all, sinless and regal. Rather, this Mary phobia—which is all too common, even among Catholics—betrays an erroneous *self*-image. Moreover, it reveals a deeper problem in the way we have appropriated the gospel of Jesus Christ. For the good news is that, even if we do go about dressed as paupers, we have royal blood coursing through our veins.

Royal Flesh

What is the truth at the heart of the gospel? Pope Leo the Great sums it up for us: "This is the gift that exceeds all others: God calls man His son, and man calls God 'Father.' "

We are children of God. This is not a metaphor, not a slogan. It is a truth that is more real than the chair you're sitting on. When we received the sacrament of baptism, we were bound by the covenant of Christ's blood into the family of God. We were raised, at that moment, to share in the eternal life of the Trinity. Listen to Saint John as he speaks of this mystery in the New Testament: "See what love the Father has given us, that we should be called children of God—and so we are" (1 Jn 3:1). *And so we are!* After so many decades of preaching the gospel, John still seemed astonished to hear himself speak those words: "we should be called children of God." Imagine, then, the evangelist's shock when he *first* heard the words Jesus spoke upon His resurrection: "I am ascending to My Father and your Father, to My God and your God" (Jn 20:17).

By baptism we have become "sons in the Son." The ancient Christians dared to call this action our *divinization*. "The Son of God became a son of man," said Saint Athanasius, "so that the sons of men might become sons of God!" After two millennia, we need—right now—to recover the early Church's sense of awe, astonishment, and gratitude for the gift at the heart of our redemption.

For we are children of God. This is the central and most profound fact about our redemption. We are not merely *forgiven;* we are *adopted* by God as sons and daughters. There's a world of difference between those two views of redemption and justification. Think about it in everyday terms: you can forgive your auto mechanic if he overcharges you; but it's unlikely that, upon forgiving him, you'll adopt him into your family. Yet that is precisely what God has done. He has forgiven us our sins so that we might find our lasting home in the family we call the Trinity.

We are children of God; by grace, we have been adopted into His family. This truth, which theologians call *divine filiation,* is present throughout the New Testament, throughout the dogmatic statements of the Church, and in every volume of systematic theology. Divine filiation is the hallmark of an authentically Catholic understanding of the gospel. Still, divine filiation remains a term most Christians are unaware of—even though it's a truth they cannot live without.

Salvation, then, is not only *from* sin, but *for* sonship—divine sonship in Christ. We are not merely forgiven by God's grace; we are adopted and divinized. That is, we "become partakers of the divine nature" (2 Pt 1:4). From the beginning, this was the life for which God created man. The sin of the first Adam and Eve was not that they desired divine life but that they desired to be divinized without God.

Yet God's will would eventually be accomplished. According to the Council of Trent, the justification of a sinner is "a translation from that state in which man is born a child of the first Adam to the state of grace and of the 'adoption of the sons' [Rom 8:15] of God through the second Adam, Jesus Christ, our Savior." Justification, according to the *Catechism,* "consists in both victory over the death caused by sin and a new participation in grace. It brings about filial adoption so that men become Christ's brethren. . . . We are brethren not by nature, but by the gift of grace, because that adoptive filiation gains us a real share in the life of the only Son, which was fully revealed in His Resurrection" (no. 654).

Fit for a King

This is the source of our royal lineage. We are children of God because of our close identification with Jesus Christ. Really, we can't get any closer to Him than we do through baptism. Pope John Paul II put it this way: "Rising from the waters of the baptismal font, every Christian hears again the voice that was once heard on the banks of the Jordan River: 'You are my beloved Son; with you I am well pleased' (Lk 3:22)." We are so closely identified with Jesus that Saint Augustine could say, "All men are one man in Christ, and the unity of Christians constitutes but one man." Augustine went on to explain that, identified with Christ, we also share his threefold mission as priest, prophet, and *king* (see 1 Pt 2:9).

Sharing His kingship, we share everything, including His mother. Read closely what Pope Pius X had to say about this:

> *For is not Mary the Mother of Christ? Then she is our Mother also. And we must in truth hold that Christ, the Word made Flesh, is also the Savior of mankind. He had a physical body like that of any other man: and again as Savior of the human family, He had a spiritual and mystical body, the society, namely, of those who believe in Christ. "We are many, but one sole body in Christ" (Rom 12:5). Now the Blessed Virgin did not conceive the Eternal Son of God merely in order that He might be made man taking His human nature from her, but also in order that by means of the nature assumed from her He might be the Redeemer of men. For which reason the Angel said to the Shepherds: "Today there is born to you a Savior Who is Christ the Lord" (Lk 2:11). Wherefore in the same holy bosom of his most chaste Mother Christ took to Himself flesh, and united to Himself the spiritual body formed by those who were to believe in Him. Hence Mary, carrying the Savior within her, may be said to have also carried all those whose life was contained in the life of the Savior. Therefore all we who are united to Christ, and as the Apostle says are*

members of His body, of His flesh, and of His bones (Eph 5:30), have issued from the womb of Mary like a body united to its head. Hence, though in a spiritual and mystical fashion, we are all children of Mary, and she is Mother of us all.

Here, Pope Pius echoes a teaching that reaches back to Saint Irenaeus (whom we discussed in Chapter 2) and so, likely, to the apostle John himself. Remember that Irenaeus described Jesus' birth as "the pure one opening purely that pure womb which regenerates men unto God."

We are made *brothers and sisters* of Christ—*adelphos,* "from the same womb." Thus we can confidently approach the queen mother of heaven not just because she condescends, in her great mercy, to hear us, but because we are her children, of royal birth, of noble blood. We can go to her not only because she is Christ's queen mother but because she is ours.

Labor Paeans

How, then, are we—in our newfound royalty—to relate to this queen mother? The Marian dogmas take us only so far; and in fact, they seem to point beyond themselves. Even the dogma most recently defined, the assumption, has a penultimate quality: now that she's in heaven, what does she *do*? We know after all what Jesus does; the book of Revelation tells us that He reigns (Rev 22:3). We know, too, what the martyrs do in heaven; the book of Revelation tells us that they pray for the satisfactory resolution of matters on earth (Rev 6:9–10).

It should be no surprise, then, that the book of Revelation tells us what Mary does in heaven. As the New Eve, the "mother of all the living," she mothers the Church, "the rest of her offspring" (Rev 12:17). Addressing the question of why the woman of Revelation is still in labor, though she is in heaven, Pope Pius X said: "What birth was it? Surely it was the birth of us who, still in exile, are yet to be generated to the perfect charity of God, and to eternal happiness. And the birth pains show the love and desire with which the Virgin from heaven above watches over us, and strives with unwearying prayer to bring about the fulfillment of the number of the elect."

Always a mother, Mary watches over us, prays for us, and leads us to fulfillment in life. The Second Vatican Council teaches:

> *This motherhood of Mary in the order of grace continues uninterruptedly from the consent which she loyally gave at*

*the Annunciation and which she sustained without wavering beneath the cross, until the eternal fulfillment of all the elect. Taken up to heaven, she did not lay aside this saving office but by her manifold intercession continues to bring us the gifts of eternal salvation. . . . Therefore the Blessed Virgin is invoked in the Church under the titles of Advocate, Helper, Benefactress, and Mediatrix. (*Lumen Gentium *62, cited in* Catechism, *no. 969)*

The Mediatrix Is the Message

You will sometimes hear non-Catholics objecting to the title "Mediatrix" applied to Mary. In my days as an evangelical, I would rush to the one Bible verse that seemed to snuff out that title: Saint Paul's categorical assertion that Christ is the "one mediator between God and man" (1 Tim 2:5). How can these two claims—Christ as the one mediator and Mary as mediatrix—be reconciled?

The apostle Paul touched upon this mystery when he stated, "We are God's coworkers" (1 Cor 3:9). If Christ is the one mediator, why would He have coworkers? Can't God get the job done by Himself? Of course He can. But since He is a Father, His job is raising up mature sons and daughters; and the way to do that is by making us coworkers.

His work is our redemption, which He shared in an unparalleled way with Mary—to whom God entrusted such tasks as feeding His Son with her own milk, singing Him to sleep, and accompanying Him all the way to the cross, where she gave her sorrowful yes to His self-offering. In short, the Father willed that His Son's entire existence as a man would hinge, so to speak, upon the ongoing consent of Mary. Can there be a more intimate coworker?

Being a disciple, a coworker with Jesus, takes effort. At times it takes suffering. One passage that seemed to have escaped my attention as a Protestant was Saint Paul's rather curious line "I rejoice in my sufferings for your sake, and in my flesh I complete what is lacking in Christ's afflictions for the sake of His body, the Church" (Col 1:24). Cradle Catholics may remember with some fondness being told (in the event of an unsuccessful team tryout, a skinned knee, or a broken heart) to "offer it up." This simple phrase holds the key that unlocks the mystery of Mary's coredemption, and ours. By consciously uniting our sufferings to our Lord's redemptive sufferings, we become coworkers. By uniting her heart to His, especially at Calvary, the Blessed Mother became the coworker par excellence.

Furthermore, the epistle to the Hebrews explains

Christ's high priesthood in terms of His being the first-born Son of God (Heb 1:1–2:17), which serves as the basis for our own divine sonship (Heb 2:10–17), as well as our priestly sanctity and service (Heb 13:10–16; see also 1 Pt 2:5). Once again, there is no tug-of-war between the Redeemer and the redeemed.

As firstborn Son in God's family, Jesus mediates as the High Priest between the Father and His children; whereas Mary mediates as queen mother and advocate (see 1 Kgs 2:19). Pope John Paul II called this her "maternal mediation." For the Father, Mary mothers the Son. For us sinners, she mothers our Savior. And for her Son, she mothers His siblings. When it comes to Mary's role in God's saving plan, "mother" is not only a noun but a verb, and hence an office.

As the Mother of God and His children, Mary shows us how to glorify the Father, not by groveling but by receiving the gift of His Son in the fullness of the Spirit. So if you want to judge how well people grasp the gospel in its essence, find out how much they make of having God as their Father—and Mary as their mother.

Abba, Not Allah

This, after all, is the essential difference in Christianity. It's not that Christians believe in only one God; there are three major monotheistic religions on earth. What makes Christianity distinctive is that Christians dare to call God "Father." In ancient Israel, the people of the old covenant spoke of God's fatherhood, but mainly in a metaphorical sense—He fathered them by providing for them and guiding them through perils.

Only Christianity can call God "Father" because only through the new covenant has God revealed Himself as a Father from all eternity. The doctrine of God the Father requires the revelation of the Trinity, because God can be an eternal Father only if there is with Him an eternal Son.

Judaism is noble because it raises believers to be good *servants* of God. The very word "Islam" literally means "submission" to Allah. But Christianity consists neither in servility nor in mere submission. Christianity consists in the love of sonship, the love of the eternal Son for the Father, the divine love in which we participate. And a loving son serves better than even the most willing and loyal slave.

I will go so far as to say that this loving sonship is possible only when believers hold to the authentically Catholic understanding of the gospel. In his book-length interview, *Crossing the Threshold of Hope,* Pope John Paul

II spoke of what happens when Christians sin or otherwise lose their sense of divine sonship: "Original sin attempts, then, to abolish fatherhood, destroying its rays which permeate the created world, placing in doubt the truth about God Who is Love and leaving man only with a sense of the master-slave relationship."

I believe the master-slave relationship—or as I prefer to think of it, the boss-worker relationship—is pervasive in Christianity today. What are its warning signs in believers? They put on their best face for God, but they never tell Him what they really think. They have what they call a personal relationship with Him, but they consider it impious to ask Him hard questions. They speak of God's sovereignty while they seethe with resentment over His demands. They scrupulously fulfill His commandments, but they have little sense of a family relationship with Him, His Church, or His mother. How, then, can they begin to call upon him as Jesus did, as "Abba," which means "Daddy"?

Taking a Contract Out

I feel a familiar ache in my heart as I say those words, because for many years I pursued such an understanding of God, salvation, and justification. As a Protestant minister and seminary professor, I followed Calvin and Luther, who read Saint Paul's letters to the Romans and the Galatians as if God were sitting as judge in a Roman courtroom, acquitting us even though He knew we were guilty, all because Christ had paid our penalty.

But the deeper I went into Romans and Galatians, the more I realized that the ancient authors were *Hebrew* before anything else. Their categories, language, and assumptions were steeped in the covenants, not in the juridical structures of the Roman empire. I had long assumed that a covenant was a legal instrument—a contract. Gradually, however, I began to wake up to something that the Catholic Church has taught from the beginning: that a covenant differs from a contract almost as much as marriage differs from prostitution. A contract exchanges property, goods and services, rights and duties; a covenant exchanges *persons.* In a contract, this product is yours and that one is mine; but in a covenant, *I* am yours and *you* are mine. Thus the covenants God makes always say the same thing: I will be your God and you will be My people—My family, My kinfolk—because covenant creates kinship.

Covenant creates family bonds that are even stronger than biological family bonds. That's something that every ancient Hebrew knew. That's what Paul knew, and John, and James. So when they heard the news that God was making a covenant with them, they knew that He was no longer merely a lawgiver or judge. He was a Father fore-most, and forever.

Bond for Glory

A strong sense of sonship—the sense that comes with deep conversion—frees us to love our mother. For as long as we cling to the master-slave relationship, we will never understand the Blessed Virgin Mary. As long as we consider ourselves God's servants or mere prisoners whom He has freed, so long we will see her as a threat to His glory. A master is glorified by his slave's servility. A master is sovereign as long as his servants grovel. But not so a father, who desires only the love of his children.

How much more true is this of the ageless Father, God Himself. God does not gain glory from our groveling; nor does He lose glory when we pay due honor to His creatures. God the Son gained not a drop of glory for Himself—after living, dying, and rising as a human being—that He had lacked beforehand. Not even God can increase that which is infinite. He came and died and rose and reigns in order to share His glory with us.

As recipients of that glory, as coheirs with Christ, as sharers in His kingship, as children of God, it's fair for us to ask: How much glory is He willing to share? And how successful will He be?

Being perfect love, He wants to share it all. But since we're finite creatures and He's the infinite creator, how could we possibly share in the fullness of divine glory? We can't do it on our own. But surely perfect love will do everything He can to give us all His glory. And, being all-powerful, He will surely succeed. Indeed, when we see Mary, we realize that He has *already* succeeded. He gave us *all* His glory by giving it to the only one who would give it to all of us: our mother.

If you come to visit my home and you give something to my small children—say, a box of candy—I can guarantee you that a fight will ensue over who gets how much. But if you give a box of chocolates as a gift to my wife, I can just as surely guarantee you that the candies will make their way to each and every child in due proportion. That, God knows, is how motherhood works.

God did not create and redeem the world in order to get more glory, but rather to share it, in due proportion, with all of us. There is no tug-of-war between the Creator and His creatures. The Father made and redeemed us through the Son and the Spirit, but He did it for our sake—starting with Mary, in whom it was accomplished not only first but best.

Do we detract from Christ's finished work by affirming its perfect realization in Mary? On the contrary, we celebrate His work, precisely by focusing our attention on the human person who manifests it most perfectly.

Mary is not God, but she is the Mother of God. She is only a creature, but she is God's greatest creation. She is not the king, but she is His chosen queen mother. Just as artists long to paint one masterpiece among their many works, so Jesus made His mother to be His greatest masterpiece. To affirm the truth about Mary does not detract from Jesus—although refusing to affirm it *does* detract from Him.

The Blessed Virgin's Merit

The problem comes when people think of divine providence in terms of human economics. What, after all, did Mary ever *do* to *earn* such honor from God? All her good works flowed from His graces. Thus all honor and glory belong to God. He owes us no graces.

If "merit" is understood as a purely economic term, then to speak of anyone meriting honors from God is untrue and offensive. But if we consider merit in a familial sense, it is as natural as an inheritance, or an allowance. In other words, as children in God's family, we merit grace as a child earns dessert—by eating everything on his plate. What father begrudges his kids the gifts he gives them? Or resents those whom he rewards? As Saint Augustine wrote: "When God rewards us for our labors, He is only crowning His work in us" (*Catechism,* no. 2006).

According to the *Catechism,* it is God's "fatherly action" that enables us to merit: "Filial adoption, in making us partakers by grace in the divine nature, can bestow *true merit* on us as a result of God's gratuitous justice. This is our right by grace, the full right of love, making us 'co-heirs' with Christ" (nos. 2008–9).

Christ has merited our capacity to merit—which He confers on us with the grace of His divine Sonship and the life of His Spirit. Indeed, Jesus did not merit a single thing for Himself, since there was nothing He needed. Thus, He merits only according to our need.

Where does God the Father show the world just how much His Son really merited? In each one of us, to be sure, but most of all in Mary. Unlike the rest of us—in whom there is often a yawning gap between what we want and what God wants—with Mary, there is no gap. The Church ascribes to Mary an unlimited capacity to merit. Far from detracting from Christ's saving work, she exemplifies it. By the gift of an infinite grace, Mary attained the goal of the covenant: a perfect interpersonal union of divine and human wills. With Mary, the ideal and the real are one and the same.

This Is a Test

Mary is the test of how well a Christian has accepted the gospel. It's not that she's the central figure of salvation history. She's not; Jesus is. But our understanding of Mary reveals everything about how we understand Jesus and His saving work.

We live our sonship best by listening to Mary and loving as she loves. Listening means responding when she says: "Do whatever He tells you." Loving means standing by Christ, even to the cross. Loving means choosing Him, in every instance, over sin.

Divine motherhood is the place where Eve and the ark are fulfilled in heaven and in your home. Divine motherhood is the place where the Church's dogmas become mother's milk for those who wish to grow in wisdom. Divine motherhood is the place where mysticism meets theology—in our heart of hearts.

Divine motherhood is the place where God wants Christians to meet Christ, their brother. I'll say it again: *adelphos* means "from the same womb." What establishes brotherhood, then, is motherhood. For Mary to have given us her Son is remarkable. But for Jesus to have given His mother to us—the very people who crucified Him and sinned against His Father—that's something great beyond imagining! After giving us His mother, we can be sure that there's nothing He would withhold.

CHAPTER 7

The Ultimate Church

Who Makes the Church a Mother?

THROUGH THE CHURCH's Scripture, Tradition, and dogma, we come to know a mother. We come to know the Blessed Virgin Mary. Yet we must be careful here. For it's not so much the Church that gives us Mary, as Mary who gives us the Church. More precisely, as Mother of the Church, she gives us her divine Son *through* the Church, and through the Church she raises new brothers and sisters to Christ.

Biblical typology leads us to see Mary as the New Eve, the mother of all the living, the mother of the covenant Family of God. Typology shows us Mary as the Bride of Christ, too. Yet, at the culmination of the scriptures, in the book of Revelation, that bride and mother is identified with the Church as well.

Revelation shows us the mystical unity between the

woman who labors to give birth to Christ (and His siblings) and the bride of the Lamb unveiled at the climax of history. The mother, the bride, the woman is Mary. The mother, the bride, the woman is the metropolis of the New Jerusalem: the Church.

Our Lady of Good Council

I said that Mary's identification with the Church is something mystical, but that does *not* mean it is metaphorical. Biblical typology is more than a mere literary convention, for the Bible is more than literature; the Bible is history. Yet typology is more than historical; it's prophetic. Still, it's more than prophecy; it's reality. And even more than reality, it's eternity. Thus, when we speak of Mary as Mother of the Church and archetype of the Church, we are speaking of a permanent truth, a *person* vividly real and a truth that's essential to God's plan for the cosmos.

The Church discussed this in a dazzling way in the documents of the Second Vatican Council (1962–65). Though this council produced no single document focused exclusively on Mary, its documents as a whole included more Marian teaching than any other ecumenical council in Church history. In fact, the Marian teaching of Vatican II outweighed that of all the previous councils combined.

Some scholars say that the council's most important document was *Lumen Gentium,* the Dogmatic Constitution on the Church. It is at the climactic moment of *Lumen Gentium* that the council fathers pronounced their most concentrated Marian teaching. The concluding section of that document is titled: "The Blessed Virgin Mary, Mother of God, in the Mystery of Christ and the Church."

"This Holy Synod," it states, "in expounding the doctrine on the Church, in which the divine Redeemer works salvation, intends to describe with diligence both the role of the Blessed Virgin in the mystery of the Incarnate Word and the Mystical Body, and the duties of redeemed mankind toward the Mother of God, who is mother of Christ and mother of men, particularly of the faithful" (*Lumen Gentium* 54).

The document then pursues a line of argument similar to the one followed in this book, examining Mary in light of theology, typology, dogma, and finally ecclesiology, the theological study of the Church. The council endorses Mary's typological foreshadowing in the Old Testament as well as her singular and essential role in the New Testament (no. 55). The discussion culminates, however, in an examination of Mary's ongoing role in the life of the Church.

Membership and Mothership

How does Mary relate to the Church?

" 'She is the mother of the members of Christ . . . having cooperated by charity that faithful might be born in the Church, who are members of that Head' " (*Lumen Gentium* 53, quoting Saint Augustine).

"The Blessed Virgin is . . . intimately united with the Church" (no. 63).

"She is . . . a preeminent and singular member of the Church" (no. 53).

She is the Church's "type and excellent exemplar in faith and charity" (no. 53).

"The Catholic Church, taught by the Holy Spirit, honors her with filial affection and piety as a most beloved mother" (no. 53).

Mary, then, is a mother to the family of God. She is a model for that family, and she actively participates in the children's "birth and education" (no. 63). As mother, she is a member of the family as, with the Father, she gives the family its particular identity.

The Church, too, is mother—but this is a function of its relation to Christ and Mary. The Church depends upon its intimate union with Mary, and the Church fulfills its own motherhood only insofar as it imitates and honors Mary's virginal motherhood.

"The Church indeed, contemplating her hidden sanctity, imitating her charity and faithfully fulfilling the Father's will, by receiving the word of God in faith becomes herself a mother." The Church, with Mary, is also a Virgin, who preserves and protects the faith that has been given to her by Jesus, her spouse. "Imitating the mother of her Lord, and by the power of the Holy Spirit, [the Church] keeps with virginal purity an entire faith, a firm hope, and a sincere charity" (no. 64).

A Glimmer of Glory

What do theologians mean, though, when they refer to Mary as an archetype? Put simply, it means that she is a type's ultimate fulfillment (see *Catechism,* nos. 967, 972).

As we've seen throughout this book, the Old Testament types foreshadowed New Testament realities. But the New Testament realities, in turn, foreshadowed heavenly glories. That's why the Book of Revelation is such an important book and the capstone of the Bible. It deals with the ultimate fulfillment of all earthly types. It shows the glory toward which God is drawing all history and all creation.

Mary is a central figure in the Apocalypse because—assumed into heaven, where she reigns—Mary is now the fulfillment of the reality of which the Church itself is merely a type. She is the Virgin and Mother, the Bride of Christ, the Heavenly Jerusalem, the metropolis that is the City of God. She is the heavenly archetype. The Church—the rest of us—must struggle toward those mystical realities during all our days on this earth.

Thus says the council:

> *While in the most holy Virgin the Church has already reached that perfection whereby she is without spot or wrinkle, the followers of Christ still strive to increase in holiness by conquering sin. And so they turn their eyes to Mary who shines forth to the whole community of the elect as the model of virtues. . . . Seeking after the glory of Christ, the Church becomes more like her exalted Type, and continually progresses in faith, hope, and charity, seeking and doing the will of God in all things. (*Lumen Gentium *65)*

Our struggle is individual, but it is communal, too. As members of God's family, we are concerned for one another and concerned to bring many others into the family. Vatican Council II holds Mary up, again, as a model of the apostolate—the model of our Christian outreach.

Indeed, our efforts at evangelization must have a Marian component. Evangelization should begin with Marian prayer and it should be suffused with Marian doctrine and devotion. For evangelization is all about building up a family, and no one can belong to a family without honoring the family's mother. Moreover, as the Second Vatican Council pointed out, Mary plays an indispensable role in each of her children's growth in holiness.

Yet how many people, even among those who are brothers of Christ, do not know they are children of Mary?

Bad for Ecumenism?

All of this brings us to the vexed question of whether Catholic doctrine on Mary is an impediment to Christian unity. Some people—even some Catholic theologians—say that we should downplay our Marian beliefs in the interest of drawing closer to Protestant churches that reject those beliefs.

To do so, however, would be counterproductive. Theology is a true science; its subject matter consists of divinely revealed mysteries. Down through the centuries, many of the doctrinal seeds that were planted by Christ and the apostles have blossomed into dogmas, as defined by the Church's magisterium. In this manner, theology has developed over time, as other sciences do.

Scientists formulate and test various theories, some of which are proven with enough certitude to be renamed laws, for instance, Newton's law of gravity; others are discarded as unworkable hypotheses. Thus, laws become the markers of scientific progress. Similarly, the definition of dogma serves as the mark of theological progress.

Dogma is the perfection of doctrine, and doctrine is nothing other than the Church's teaching and preaching the gospel truth, as Jesus commissioned and empowered her to do. When the pope chooses to define a Marian dogma, he does much more than teach the world a valuable lesson in theology. He uses his God-given charism to fulfill his apostolic mission to preach the gospel to all nations (see Mt 28:18–20).

Throughout the history of the Church, the definition of dogmas has stimulated the apostolic and theological energies of some of her best minds, *especially* when a definition became the occasion of controversy. In the 1940s, many Protestants, including the late Max Thurian of Taizé, France, objected strenuously after hearing rumors that Pope Pius XII was about to define the dogma of Mary's assumption. "Where is that in the Bible?" they asked, as they made dire predictions about the death of Catholic ecumenism.

Yet the definition of the assumption coincided with the dawn of a golden age of Catholic ecumenism. Now, almost fifty years later, the Catholic Church can be described as the engine of the ecumenical movement, when many of the institutions of the old guard have lost their steam.

And incidentally, Max Thurian died a Catholic priest on the feast of the Assumption in 1996.

Authentic ecumenical progress is not simply the result of our own human energies. Even more, it is not caused by compromise on either side. "Here it is not a question of altering the deposit of faith," wrote Pope John Paul II, "changing the meaning of dogmas, eliminating essential words from them, accommodating truth to the preferences of a particular age. . . . The unity willed by God can be attained only by the adherence of all to the content of revealed faith in its entirety" (*Ut Unum Sint* 18).

Ecumenical unity thus requires a special grace and the Word of God, who acts for the sake of His family. Accordingly, we should not expect Him to work apart from, but *through,* the mother He gave us to serve as the symbol and source—the archetype—of family unity.

And in the End

Whatever our disagreements, these are family matters more than political issues. Indeed, we all should resist the temptation to reduce such matters to ecclesiastical politics or apologetic debates, or to respond to our honest differences by impugning motives. How wrongheaded it is to strive after Mary's honor in a way that would dishonor her.

While I am not naive in matters ecumenical, I am hopeful, but only because of the Father's desire to pour out His supernatural power to unite all of His children around His Son and "our common mother" (*Redemptoris Mater* 25).

This, after all, is what we learn from the typology of the Bible, illuminated by the Church's dogma. The eternal reality that has been prophesied—the communion toward which human history has been moving as its dramatic conclusion—is the cosmic, corporate, human expression of what God did in Mary, making her bride, making her mother, making her the archetype of a Church that must include us all.

CHAPTER 8

A Concluding Unapologetic Postscript

NOW THAT YOU'VE read most of this book on the Blessed Virgin Mary, perhaps you're looking forward to speaking with friends, family members, or coworkers who are Christians, but perhaps doubters when it comes to Marian doctrine. If you're eager to evangelize, then I'm pleased. I wrote this book so that my fellow Catholics would never be ashamed of their supernatural mother as I was once ashamed of my natural mother when she came to take me home from school.

Yet I'd also like to raise a caution, and urge you not to be too eager—or rather, not to be eager for the wrong reasons. I urge you never to forget that, when you defend the Blessed Virgin, you're defending your mother, not a quarterback, not a goal line. You should defend her only as she would want to be defended. No mother worth the name wants her children to go on the offensive in defending her. No mother worth the name wants her children to be rude in defending her. No mother worth the name wants to be the subject of a schoolyard brawl.

I say this because I sometimes encounter people who practice apologetics as a full-contact sport or as take-no-prisoners warfare. For such apologists, the goal is to win the argument, even if that means utterly humiliating their "enemies."

That is no way to prove Marian doctrines. Children of Mary have no enemies. We know only our brothers and sisters in Jesus Christ—our *adelphoi,* from the same womb. We need not so much argue them back home (though arguments are sometimes necessary) as love them home (though love can sometimes be tough).

Moreover, we must never grow overly proud that we have come to recognize ourselves as children of the queen mother. We must never come to believe that we have all the answers. Though the answers are all available to us, no one is ever in full possession of them. God will continue to humble us, to remind us that we're children, by allowing us to fall and to find ourselves without the right answer at the right moment. He'll even permit this when we are, ostensibly, working for His good cause.

I can vouch for all of this, because, shortly after my conversion, God brought the message home to me.

I HAD LONG since begun to feel at home in the Catholic Church, and I was elated by how enthusiastically Catholics were receiving my conversion testimony wherever I went. Fundamentalists and evangelicals would sometimes attend my lectures to challenge me, but I was eager to take them on. I knew the arguments before they even opened their mouths—I had once espoused them myself—and I knew exactly the right biblical response. I even began to look forward to these challenges, as a marksman looks forward to the next clay pigeon. I was feeling very much the macho apologist.

Flush with so many successes, I found myself one weekend in the neighborhood of my old Protestant seminary, Gordon-Conwell. I decided to go back and spend some time with the professor I'd served as a teaching assistant. He seemed eager to see me and even invited me to stay at his home while I was in town. He had heard, of course, about my entering the Catholic Church, and he was, to put it mildly, disappointed. He said he was looking forward to discussing the matter at greater length.

I knew that he wanted to challenge me, and I was eager to be challenged.

I arrived, and we greeted each other warmly; but my initial hunch was right. It wasn't long before my host and his wife began to pepper me with all kinds of questions about the pope, purgatory, the Eucharist, the priesthood, confession . . . All of which was fine by me, because, through a whole day and into the night, I was like an all-star slugger at batting practice, slamming one slow pitch after another into the bleachers.

Then, around midnight, just as I was beginning to look forward to some well-earned shut-eye, my friend said to me: "What about the assumption?"

I knew what he was implying—that there is no scriptural evidence for the assumption. I was tired, and annoyed that he was bringing up the assumption at that late hour of the night. But I was also unprepared. I replied, "Well, you can look at Revelation 12 and see that there she was, body and soul in heaven."

"That's nice, Scott," he said. "But give me evidence that anyone in the Church believed that before the sixth century."

I responded that, in all its history, the Church had

never honored a tomb as the final resting place of Mary's bones.

He pointed out, rightly, that the argument from silence was about as weak an argument as one could offer.

I acknowledged that he was right, but countered that times of persecution rarely yield evidence of doctrine or devotion. Survival and perseverance are the Church's top priorities.

My hosts were not impressed.

And the macho apologist was beginning to feel the effects of a day's worth of sporting arguments—and a year's worth of intellectual pride.

I scrambled to point out that, yes, it's not until the sixth century that the assumption makes its debut in our documentary history—but by then, we encounter it as established and developed, with its own feast days, hymns, and literature. When the emperor declared it a universal feast, there was not even a hint of resistance or controversy.

My hosts smiled. "That's all well and good, Scott. But the fact is that you don't have anything to account for five centuries of silence, do you?"

Up to this point, our discussion had been amiable. But now I felt it turn somewhat pointed, almost adversarial.

But I had to respond, "No, I can't think of anything."

"Can you recommend a book? Anything at all that I might read?"

I shook my head.

"You don't have answers from the first five centuries. You don't have a book I can read—*you,* who have a book for everything, don't have a book on the assumption!" He was just savoring the moment, relishing this victory.

I said, "No."

"Let me remind you, Scott, that this is a dogma, *infallibly defined*. And you can't explain to me why there was silence for five centuries?"

"I don't know," I said.

It was the closing moment of a dramatic exchange that had gone on for hours, and all my previous triumphs seemed reduced to nothing. I kind of limped up the steps to my guest room bed, feeling like I'd let my mother down.

I sat on the bed, then dropped to my knees and prayed an apology to Jesus. I felt I'd let Him down by letting His mother down. I felt as if I'd run with the ball to the one-yard line, only to fumble short of the goal. I said, "I'm sorry, Lord, for my weakness and failure." I prayed a Hail Mary. Then I fell, exhausted, to sleep.

They let me sleep in. I woke up at nine, and a plate of scrambled eggs awaited me in the kitchen.

As I sat down and began eating, I noticed that the calendar said Monday, December 8. Something about that date set off an alarm in my memory. Was it a holy day? Then I remembered it was the feast of the Immaculate Conception, my first as a Catholic—and I had almost missed it, staying, as I was, in Protestant territory.

I sheepishly said to my hostess, "Um, today is a holy day of obligation. Is there any way I can get to, uh, Mass somewhere close by?"

She said, "Oh, you're in luck. Saint Paul's is in our backyard." She even called to find out their Mass times—but they had just finished their last Mass for the day. So she proceeded to call around ten nearby churches, without finding a single one that could accommodate me before my flight out of town. Finally she discovered a listing for a Carmelite chapel at Peabody shopping mall, around fifteen miles away.

One more call and she found out that, indeed, the chapel had a noon Mass. There would be just enough time for me to get there, get back to the house, and have my hosts drive me to the airport.

So I got ready for my departure and left for the mall, arriving just a little before noon. I asked directions to the chapel and soon found myself in a crowd of Christmas shoppers making their way down a narrow staircase to the basement. At bottom, I found myself amid a standing-room-only congregation, and I took my place in the back.

A bell rang, and an old priest sauntered out. He must have been in his seventies. And I thought, Oh, no, this is gonna be a long Mass.

Through the first parts of the Mass, I found myself glancing frequently at my watch, thinking anxiously about my flight.

When it came to the homily, though, everything changed. That ancient man stepped up to the pulpit and looked out at us. Surely everyone could see there was a gleam in his eye. He seemed to be speaking directly to me when he said, "We're celebrating our *mother* today!"

From there he took off, preaching a firestorm. Billy Graham had nothing on this guy. "If anybody should ask you," he thundered, " 'Why do you believe that Mary was conceived without sin?' what are you gonna tell him?" He paused.

"What are you gonna tell him?" He paused again.

Then, with a twinkle, he said, "Tell him this: If you could have created your mother and preserved her from original sin, would you? Would you? . . . Of course you would!

"But *could* you? No, you couldn't! But Jesus could and so Jesus did!"

Afterward, I had a hard time concentrating on the Mass, but I surely wasn't thinking about my flight out of town. I wanted to talk with this priest.

When the Mass had ended, the crowd returned to its shopping, and I made my way back to the chapel's small sacristy. "Father, do you have a minute?" I asked.

"No," he replied without looking up.

I said, "Do you have half a minute?"

Finally, he looked up at me. "What do you want?"

I said, "I'm a grad of Gordon-Conwell, top of my class, but I just converted earlier this year."

He smiled at me as he said, "Gordon-Conwell, up in South Hamilton—I used to teach there. I taught theology."

I said, "No, I don't think you understand. It's an evangelical Protestant seminary."

He raised an eyebrow. "No, young man, I don't think you understand. It used to be a Carmelite seminary, and I taught there for decades. . . . When did you graduate?"

"Eighty-two," I replied. "Top of my class, a stalwart Calvinist. I converted. Now I'm back to visit, and it's really humbling."

"Ha!" he said. "We give them our seminary; they give us their graduates. Seems like a fair exchange."

Then he remembered how our conversation had started. "So what's your question?"

I told him the whole story of the previous day, culminating in the humiliation at midnight. "You were so good in your homily, I was wondering whether you might know a book I can recommend."

"There's a good reason why you can't think of any titles," he said. "There aren't any titles in print. There was one, and it just went out of print last week."

I was astonished. "You really know your Marian bibliography, Father."

He said, "In this case, I should. I wrote the book."

My jaw dropped. I felt as if I'd entered the Twilight Zone.

"Yes, I wrote it. It's called *The Assumption of Mary,* and I was just notified last week that it was going out of print . . . But I have two copies." He reached into a cabinet. "What is this professor's name?"

I told him.

"And you, you're married, what's your wife's name?"

"Kimberly."

And he inscribed the books with his name—Father Kilian Healy, O.Carm.—for my wife and for my friends.

Then he left abruptly and left me astonished. I drove back to my friends' house, marveling at God's mercy.

I pulled up with just enough time to load the car and get to Logan Airport. My former professor couldn't ride along because he was teaching that afternoon. So we were standing in the driveway saying good-bye.

I said to him, "One last thing. You asked about a book about the assumption of Mary." I reached into my pocket for Father Healy's book as, in thirty seconds, I summarized the episode at the chapel. Breathlessly I explained that this was the only book available, and it had just gone out of print, and I had just happened to run into the author at the mall that afternoon.

He was speechless. His wife just laughed as she drove me off to the airport.

As I got on the plane, I felt like a little boy. I pictured Mary patting me on the head and saying, "Don't worry so much about defending me. Just love me and love my Son, and where you fall short, we'll make up for what you lack."

WHEN ALL MY research and rhetoric had failed, when I was thoroughly humiliated according to my own human standards, when I could do no more, then I did what I should have done from the start. I prayed a Hail Mary.

That prayer at the end of the day, in my moment of utter weakness and humiliation, was the turning point in this episode of my life. It set into motion a chain of events that I couldn't have surpassed with my best-prepared speeches.

When it comes to explaining the Blessed Virgin Mary, having a lot of love is more important than having a lot of answers. When we come up lacking, she'll make greater goods out of our deficiencies, as only a mother can do. Whenever we're humiliated and shown our weakness, we should get ready for something better than we could ever plan and prepare to accomplish.

Evangelize with joy, then, and with confidence. Know from the start that you don't have all the answers—but your Savior does, and He loves His mother. He will give you everything you need, even if sometimes you need to fail.

APPENDIX
The Venerable Beads

GIVEN THE OPPORTUNITY to praise our mothers—at birthday parties and wedding anniversaries, or in eulogies—we sons can get long-winded, because we find ourselves inexorably drawn back to our earliest years. We feel we have to recapture those childhood days with Mom and, in remembering them aloud, make up for all the moments when we were less than grateful for her care, less than loving in response to her love.

In beginning to write this book, I struggled to set down memories that are somewhat painful for me, including the time when, in ignorance and misguided zeal, I destroyed my late grandmother's rosary. Perhaps, in composing this appendix, I am trying to make things right. I cannot repair those beads that belonged to Grandma Hahn. They went out with the day's trash almost thirty years ago. I can, however, make reparation. I can make it up to that matriarch of my family, even as I make it up to heaven's queen mother, whom my grandmother loved.

Let Me Count the Ways

Down through the millennia, Christians have expressed their love for the Blessed Virgin in many different ways. The early Christians made pilgrimage to the sites associated with her life. The Eastern churches influenced by Byzantium composed long "akathist" hymns in her honor. The Ethiopians developed a rich tradition of liturgical prayer to Mary. The Egyptians appear first in the documentary record with the prayer *Sub Tuum Praesidium*. The West, in turn, produced the "Hail, Holy Queen," the *Memorare,* and many litanies. Both East and West have amassed a stunning heritage of Marian art—predominantly icons in the East, and both sculpture and paintings in the West.

Without a doubt, though, the Church's most popular and beloved expression of Marian devotion is the rosary. It's my favorite expression, too.

The rosary consists of a certain sequence of prayers that we recite aloud while we meditate on scenes (or *mysteries*) from the life of Jesus and Mary. There are fifteen mysteries in all.

THE JOYFUL MYSTERIES

The Annunciation (Lk 1:26–38): The angel Gabriel tells Mary she will conceive the Messiah.

The Visitation (Lk 1:39–56): Mary visits her kinswoman Elizabeth.

The Nativity (Mt 1:18–25; Lk 2:1–20): Jesus is born.

The Presentation (Lk 2:22–38): Mary and Joseph go to the temple to dedicate Jesus to God.

The Finding of the Child Jesus (Lk 2:41–51): During a pilgrimage to the temple, Jesus is separated from Mary and Joseph.

THE SORROWFUL MYSTERIES

The Agony in the Garden (Mt 26:36–46): Jesus prays to be spared His suffering.

The Scourging (Mt 27:26): Jesus is whipped by the Romans.

The Crowning with Thorns (Mt 27:29): The Romans ridicule Jesus' kingship.

The Carrying of the Cross (Jn 19:17).

The Crucifixion (Mk 15:22–38): Jesus dies on the cross.

THE GLORIOUS MYSTERIES

The Resurrection (Mt 28:1–10): Jesus rises from the dead.

The Ascension (Lk 24:50–51): Jesus returns to the Father.

The Descent of the Holy Spirit (Acts 2): The first Christian Pentecost.

The Assumption of Mary (Rev 11:19–12:1): Mary is taken, body and soul, to heaven.

The Coronation (Rev 12:1). Mary is crowned queen of heaven and earth.

While we meditate on these mysteries, we usually count out our recited prayers on the set of beads, which also bears the name "rosary"—a word whose root meaning is a "garland of roses."

With each mystery, we recite one Our Father and ten Hail Marys, followed by a Glory Be. Together these prayers make up one *decade* of the rosary. While a full rosary consists of all fifteen decades, Christians usually pray only one set of five mysteries at a time. In its official documents, the Church defines the recitation of the rosary as the recitation of five decades.

Hearts and Hands and Voices

Non-Catholics will sometimes dismiss the rosary as a mindless, mechanical droning of formulas. Some will even condemn the practice, citing Jesus' rejection of "vain repetition" in prayer (Mt 6:7). But nothing could be further from the mark.

First, the rosary is anything but mindless. Indeed, its meditative technique has been refined by centuries of practice in order to engage the mind most completely. The rosary ordinarily engages at least three of our senses—with the sound of voices, the feeling of beads, and the sight of devotional images—so that those senses themselves are made prayerful. Thus committed, body and soul, to prayer, we are less prone to distraction.

Further, the formulas themselves are rich in scriptural doctrine and devotion. The Our Father we learn from the lips of Jesus Himself. The Hail Mary comes from the words of Gabriel and Elizabeth in Luke's gospel. And who could argue with the words of the Glory Be, which merely give praise to the eternal and Blessed Trinity?

There's usually a very simple mistake at the root of these critiques of Catholic prayer. Somehow, many Christians have gotten hold of the idea that *formal* prayer is bad and that prayer, in order to be true, must be spontaneous, creative, and emotional. Yet Jesus did not teach this. In fact, He Himself used the formal prayer of ancient Israel (see Mk 12:29; 15:34; Jn 7:10–14).

Jesus did condemn vain repetition, but not all repetition is vain. I remember watching a Christian rock musician field questions from people who just couldn't understand his conversion to Catholicism. One woman asked, "How do you deal with all the vain repetition?"

He looked at her with the most loving smile and said, "I don't mind repetition. I'm a bass player. It's my livelihood."

Repetition and routine can be very good for us and for our relationships. My wife never tires of hearing me say, "I love you." My mother never tires of hearing me thank her for my upbringing. My adversaries never tire of hearing me say I'm sorry for my mistakes. God, too, never tires of hearing us repeat the set phrases that have been hallowed for prayer by scripture and Christian tradition. Non-Catholics know this, too, and so we hear all kinds of Christians echo the words "Amen!" "Alleluia!" and "Praise the Lord!"

Tradition sets certain phrases because they sum up a particular thought or feeling. Moreover, they tend to clarify the thought or intensify the feeling not only in the hearer but in the speaker as well. The more I tell my wife I love her, the more I fall in love with her. The more I speak my thanks to my mother, the more I must ponder my gratitude to her.

The more, in turn, we give our voices, our hands, and

our hearts to words of love for our queen, our mother, and her Son, the more we will grow in devotion and holiness.

How the Rosary Arose

No area of Christian life is so susceptible to fads and fashion as the techniques of prayer. This is true not only for Catholics. I saw it throughout my years as a Presbyterian minister, too. Pop methods come and go at a rate of several per decade. Yet the rosary has persevered through many centuries, enduring a full frontal assault in the years of the Reformation. From generation to generation, it has won the approval of all the popes and the most revered of the faithful: Saint Thomas Aquinas, Saint Alphonsus Liguori, Louis Pasteur, Fulton Sheen, and Mother Teresa of Calcutta, to name just a few.

Where did it all begin? It's almost impossible to say. Legend has it that Mary herself appeared to Saint Dominic Guzman, the founder of the Dominicans, handed him the beads, and taught him to pray. Indeed, Dominic and his order do deserve most of the credit for the spread of the devotion in the High Middle Ages.

History, however, indicates that Christians were reciting the rosary even before Dominic was born. The prayer probably developed gradually over centuries. Believers in the East had the habit of counting their prayers on strings of beads or knotted strings. Monks used these strings to keep count as they recited all of the Bible's 150 psalms.

Simple Christians, many of whom couldn't read, adapted the practice by substituting 150 recitations of other prayers. Thus, this practice was sometimes called the poor man's psalter. The prayer most often chosen was the Hail Mary, recited over fifteen rounds of ten.

The Protestant historian Anne Winston-Allen has shown that the rosary was a profoundly Christ-centered devotion and the most potent force "for spiritual renewal and reform on the eve of the Reformation."

Why do we know so little of the origins of the rosary? Because it arose out of love.

Notice how, when movies flash back to scenes of tender love, the camera turns to soft focus. History works the same way. Humankind records its horrors in the minutest detail, but love is most often left to perpetuate itself through love. Christian history works with precision, for example, in recounting the deaths and torments of the martyrs; but history leaves us few and sparse accounts of the love of Christian mothers. Yet can we doubt that, in every generation, mothers have produced as many Christians as martyrs did?

Though the roots of the rosary are obscured deep in the ground of history, its fruits are evident throughout the Christian centuries, including our own.

And its varieties are endless. In my country, most people begin with the Sign of the Cross, then proceed to pray the Apostles' Creed while holding the crucifix at the end of their beads. Next, they pray an Our Father, three Hail Marys, and a Glory Be, for an increase in faith, hope, and charity. Then they pray the mysteries. Some people have the custom of reciting the Fatima Prayer—so called because it was revealed by Mary to three peasant children in Fatima, Portugal, in 1917—after each Glory Be. After the last mystery, many people will recite the "Hail, Holy Queen," the Litany of Loreto, or some other Marian prayer.

Upping the Meds

The *how* of the rosary is not too difficult to pick up—the fingering of the beads, the repetition of the words. Its simplicity has made it popular among the most immense variety of people.

Where most people get hung up is in the meditation. The mysteries are what make the rosary. When we repeat the formal prayers, we try to focus our mind and heart upon the given event from the life of Jesus. We try to place ourselves within the scene, imagining what it was like to be there.

This is the stuff of the rosary. Yet this is where we will be most prone to distraction. Once we open the corral of our imagination, there's no telling which horses will run loose—or how far afield they'll go.

That's why I always recommend scripture as the foundation of all rosary meditation. There are many fine collections of scriptural meditations on the mysteries of the rosary. Such books are wonderful, and the Holy Spirit can use them to open our minds to deeper wisdom and to turn our hearts to repentance. Some small books give a single, well-chosen line for us to digest with each Hail Mary. Others give fully developed chapters for us to read as we begin a mystery or as we go along.

Still, when I speak of a scriptural rosary, I mean much more than a booklet, more than a book, and even more than a library full of books. I mean that Catholics should immerse themselves in scripture so that each mystery of the rosary evokes *countless* biblical associations, from both the Old and the New Testaments. For the mysteries—the events of Jesus' life—did not arise out of nothing. God has been preparing each of them from all eternity. I have tried to make that point clear throughout this book, showing, for example, that the last of the mysteries, the coronation, was implicit in the garden of Eden at the beginning of time, and that the mystery of the annunciation was foreshadowed there, too. In Chapter 3, we saw that Mary's visitation to Elizabeth was the fulfillment of the Old Testament odyssey of the ark of the covenant.

If we steep ourselves in scripture, we will draw from rich reservoirs, again, when we meditate upon the third glorious mystery, the first Pentecost. We will think first, of course, of the action-packed scene in the Acts of the Apostles. But we will also think of the Pentecost of ancient Israel, marking the giving of the Law. We will recall the time when the Holy Spirit descended upon the elders in the desert (see Num 11:24–29). When we imagine the tongues of fire, we will recall how Elijah called fire from heaven to consume his sacrifice (1 Kgs 18:24–38). What, then, is the new covenant sacrifice consumed by the fire of the Holy Spirit? Could it be you and me? Then, when the apostles speak in tongues, we will naturally remember the story of the Tower of Babel (Gen 11) and the passage in Isaiah (28:11) when God again confused the speech of the people. What does it mean that, on Pentecost, He reversed the process?

" 'Seek in reading,' " says the *Catechism,* " 'and you

will find in meditating' " (no. 2654, quoting Guigo the Carthusian).

This entire book is only the smallest hint of where we can go in our meditations when we're well prepared by sustained, disciplined, and prayerful study of the Bible. Put simply: we have to read the scriptures every day; we have to receive the scriptures often in the context of the liturgy; we have to read the meditations and commentaries of the Fathers and the saints; and we have to pray the scriptures in the Spirit.

In the midst of such a life, our every rosary will be a scriptural rosary, flowing from our heart to Mary's to Christ's—and back again. Read the Bible, then; pray the rosary; and find your place in the living history of the people of God, stretching from Adam to Israel, through Christ to the Church to you.

Will the Circle Be Unbroken?

Love engendering love—that's the history of the rosary, and that's the secret of the rosary.

Pray the rosary! This is what I urge Catholics and all Christians of goodwill. Pray the rosary, and realize that every recitation is plugging you into the permanent things, taking you out of the transitory and ephemeral, the things that matter most to people who really don't know what matters.

Put time aside to pray the rosary in a concentrated, dedicated way. But pray the rosary again when you find time that would otherwise be badly spent—when you're stuck in a doctor's waiting room or delayed in rush-hour traffic. The rush hour is unreal in comparison to the reality you're praying, the mysteries of ultimate reality. Your beads and your prayers are more real than the cars in front of you and the horns that are honking.

Once I looked down with disgust upon a string of rosary beads. I saw it as a noose that choked off true devotion in countless Roman Catholics. When I held Grandma Hahn's rosary, I couldn't break that loop quickly or forcefully enough.

Now, when I look down at my own beads, I see the same circle, but it is different. It suggests a queen's crown, a mother's encircling arms.

SOURCES AND REFERENCES

15 *The newborn's eyes:* See Herbert Ratner, M.D., "The Natural Institution of the Family," *Child and Family* 20 (1988): 89–106.

19 *"God in His deepest mystery":* Pope John Paul II, *Puebla: A Pilgrimage of Faith* (Boston: Daughters of St. Paul, 1979), 86. See also Antoine E. Nachef, *The Mystery of the Trinity in the Theological Thought of Pope John Paul II* (New York: Peter Lang, 1999), 49–62; Bertrand de Margerie, S.J., *The Christian Trinity in History* (Still River, Mass.: St. Bede's Publications, 1982), 274–324.

23 On typology and the literal and spiritual senses of scripture, see Mark Shea, *Making Senses Out of Scripture: Reading the Bible as the First Christians Did* (San Diego: Basilica Press, 1999); Ignace de la Potterie, S.J., "The

Spiritual Sense of Scripture," *Communio* 23 (1996): 738–56; William Kurz, S.J., and Kevin Miller, "The Use of Scripture in the *Catechism of the Catholic Church,*" *Communio* 23 (1996): 480–507; Pontifical Biblical Commission, *The Interpretation of the Bible in the Church* (Boston: St. Paul Books, 1993), 81–109; Leonhard Goppelt, *Typos: The Typological Interpretation of the Old Testament in the New* (Grand Rapids, Mich.: Eerdmans, 1982); R. M. Davidson, *Typology in Scripture* (Berrien Springs, Mich.: Andrews University Press, 1982); G. W. H. Lampe and K. J. Woollcombe, *Essays on Typology* (London: SCM Press, 1957); Jean Daniélou, S.J., *The Bible and the Liturgy* (Notre Dame, Ind.: University of Notre Dame Press, 1956).

24 *Saint Joseph's role:* Raymond Brown, S.S., *The Birth of the Messiah* (Garden City, N.Y.: Doubleday, 1977), 29.

26 *What is a covenant?:* On the familial nature of covenant relations and obligations in ancient Israel, see Frank Moore Cross, "God as Divine Kinsman: What Covenant Meant in Ancient Israel," *Biblical Archaeology Review,* July/August 1999, 32–33, 60; idem, "Kinship and Covenant in Ancient Israel," in *From Epic to Canon: History and Literature in Ancient Israel* (Baltimore: Johns

Hopkins University Press, 1998), 3–21; Scott Hahn, *A Father Who Keeps His Promises: God's Covenant Love in Scripture* (Ann Arbor: Servant, 1998); idem, "Kinship by Covenant: A Biblical-Theological Study of Covenant Types and Texts in the Old and New Testaments" (Ph.D. dissertation, Marquette University, 1995); Paul Kalluveettil, *Declaration and Covenant* (Rome: Pontifical Biblical Institute Press, 1982), 212; D. J. McCarthy, S.J., *Old Testament Covenant: A Survey of Current Opinions* (Richmond, Va.: John Knox Press, 1972), 33.

27 *If God is family, heaven is home:* On the Catholic view of justification as our supernatural participation in Christ's divine Sonship, see the *Catechism of the Catholic Church*, nos. 1996–97, and Session 6, Chapter 4, of the Council of Trent, in H. J. Schroeder, O.P., ed., *Canons and Decrees of the Council of Trent* (London: B. Herder, 1941), 31. See also Richard A. White, "Justification as Divine Sonship" in *Catholic for a Reason: Scripture and the Mystery of the Family of God* (Steubenville, Ohio: Emmaus Road, 1998), 88–105; M. J. Scheeben, *The Mysteries of Christianity* (St. Louis: Herder, 1950), 623–24.

32 *The motif of the New Adam:* On the notion of narrative time in the gospel of John, see R. A. Culpepper,

Anatomy of the Fourth Gospel: A Study in Literary Design (Philadelphia: Fortress Press, 1983), 53–75.

35 *"what have you to do with Me?":* For other examples, see 1 Kgs 19:20; Gn 23:15; Lk 8:26–39; Mt 8:28–34; Mk 1:23–28; Lk 4:31–37; Mk 5. See also M. Miguens, *Mary, "The Servant of the Lord": An Ecumenical Proposal* (Boston: Daughters of St. Paul, 1978), 109–29; Thor Strandenaes, "John 2:4 in a Chinese Cultural Context: Unnecessary Stumbling Block for Filial Piety?" in T. Fornberg and D. Hellholm, eds., *Texts and Contexts: Biblical Texts in Their Textual and Situational Contexts* (Oslo: Scandinavian University Press, 1995), 956–78.

40 *"Christ became man":* Justin, *Dialogue* 100. See discussions in Johannes Quasten, *Patrology,* vol. 1, (Allen, Tex.: Christian Classics, 1952), 211–12; Luigi Gambero, *Mary and the Fathers of the Church* (San Francisco: Ignatius Press, 1999), 44–48.

42 *Perhaps, again, it was the influence:* See John Henry Cardinal Newman, *The Mystical Rose* (Princeton, N.J.: Scepter, 1996), 20.

42 *"became incarnate"*: Quoted in Quasten, *Patrology,* vol. 1, 296.

42 *"The knot of Eve's disobedience":* Irenaeus, *Against the Heresies* 3.22.3.

42 *"If the former [Eve] disobeyed":* Ibid., 5.19.1.

43 *Here, Irenaeus's discussion: Proof of the Apostolic Teaching* 33.

43 *Finally, Irenaeus extends: Against the Heresies* 4.33.11, quoted in Quasten, *Patrology,* vol. 1, 299.

43 *Justin in Ephesus:* Newman, *Mystical Rose,* 20. See also Lucien Deiss, C.S.Sp., *Mary, Daughter of Zion* (Collegeville, Minn.: Liturgical Press, 1972), 129.

44 *"For it was while Eve":* Tertullian, *On the Flesh of Christ* 17.

52 *the first Jewish readers:* M. Barker, *The Older Testament* (London: SPCK, 1987), 221: "In the popular Judaism of Roman times, the menorah was universally employed

as its symbol, and yet the Rabbis forbade its use. It was forbidden to make a menorah like the one in the temple; lamps with five, six, or eight branches were permitted, but a lamp with seven branches was not."

55 *"The image of the woman":* Newman, *Mystical Rose,* 21.

60 *the anguish of the woman's delivery:* Deiss, *Mary*, 140.

64 *"It is sometimes asked":* Newman, *Mystical Rose,* 23.

65 *"because she is mother":* Quoted in Thomas Livius, *The Blessed Virgin in the Fathers of the First Six Centuries* (London: Burns and Oates, 1893), 271.

65 *"The Virgin Mary is":* Ephrem, *The Pearl,* quoted ibid., 268.

66 *"signifies Mary":* Quoted in Livius, *Blessed Virgin,* 269.

66 *"reproduces the mystery":* Deiss, *Mary,* 142.

67 *"The holy apostle would not":* Newman, *Mystical Rose,* 20.

67 *The woman of the Apocalypse must:* See Bernard J. Lefrois, S.V.D., *The Woman Clothed with the Sun: Individual or Collective* (Rome: Orbis Catholicus, 1954), 255–62.

80 *This confirms what we know:* See George Kirwin, "The Nature of the Queenship of Mary" (Ph.D. dissertation, Catholic University of America, 1973), 300. See also Edward Sri, "Treat Her Like a Queen: The Biblical Call to Honor Mary as Royal Mother," in Leon Supprenant, ed., *Catholic for a Reason II: Scripture and the Mystery of the Mother of God* (Steubenville, Ohio: Emmaus Road, 2000), 81–97. For more on the institution of the queen mother in the Davidic kingdom and ancient Near Eastern dynasties, see Carol Smith, "Queenship in Israel: The Cases of Bathsheba, Jezebel and Athaliah," in John Day, ed., *King and Messiah in Israel and the Ancient Near East* (Sheffield: Sheffield Academic Press, 1998), 142–62; K. Spanier, "The Queen Mother in the Judaean Royal Court," in A. Brenner, ed., *A Feminist Companion to Samuel and Kings* (Sheffield: Sheffield Academic Press, 1994), 186–95; S. Ackerman, "The Queen Mother and the Cult in Ancient Israel," *Journal of Biblical Literature* 112 (1993): 385–401; Z. Ben-Barak, "The Status and Right of the Gebira," *Journal of Biblical Literature* 110 (1991): 23–34; George Montague, S.M., *Our Father, Our Mother: Mary*

and the Faces of God (Steubenville, Ohio: Franciscan University Press, 1990), 89–101; N. Andreasen, "The Role of the Queen Mother in Israelite Society," *Catholic Biblical Quarterly* 45 (1982): 174–94.

91 *What is dogma?:* See Joseph Cardinal Ratzinger, "Crisis in Catechetics," *Canadian Catholic Review*, June 1983, 178.

94 *"David her forefather":* In M. F. Toal, ed., *Sunday Sermons of the Great Fathers,* vol. IV (Chicago: Henry Regnery, 1963), 426.

95 *"If Eve was raised":* Newman, *Mystical Rose,* 11.

95 *"Mary was no mere instrument":* Ibid., 58.

96 *Saint Ephrem of Syria: Nisibene Songs* 27.8.

96 *All have sinned, said Augustine: De Natura et Gratia* 42.

97 *"that the most Blessed Virgin Mary": Ineffabilis Deus.*

99 *As early as the third century:* Gambero, *Mary and the Fathers,* 69–70.

102 *Saint Thomas Aquinas summed it up: Summa Theologica* III, xxviii, a. 2, quoted in Donalds Attwater, *A Dictionary of Mary* (New York: P. J. Kenedy and Sons, 1956), 299.

105 *This is a classic example:* Saint Jerome's refutation appears in most editions of the Church Fathers as "Against Helvidius." Other commentators note that "come together," in Greek, could apply to domestic arrangements (e.g., sharing a house) as well as sexual arrangements. Moreover, the Greek word for "until" does not imply what the English word *until* implies. Thus, a Greek historian could write: "Not a soldier perished until they reached safety."

106 On the tacit reference to a previous vow of virginity implied in Mary's response to Gabriel, see Geoffrey Graystone, S.M., "Virgin of All Virgins: The Interpretation of Luke 1:34" (S.S.D. dissertation, Pontifical Biblical Commission, Rome, 1968).

107 *clear from scripture and Tradition:* On the physical integrity of Mary's virginal condition, prepartum and postpartum, see *Catechism of the Catholic Church,* nos. 499, 510. See also Saint John of Damascus, *Orthodox Faith* 4.15;

Manuel Miguens, O.F.M., *The Virgin Birth: An Evaluation of Scriptural Evidence,* 2nd ed. (Boston: St. Paul Editions, 1981).

107 *Saint Epiphanius dismissed:* Gambero, *Mary and the Fathers,* 123. For an evangelical Protestant scholar's defense of Saint Epiphanius's view, namely, that Jesus was called "son of Mary" to distinguish him from Saint Joseph's other children by his first (deceased) wife, see Richard Bauckham, "The Brothers and Sisters of Jesus: An Epiphanian Response to John P. Meier," *Catholic Biblical Quarterly* 56 (1994): 686–700; idem, *Jude and the Relatives of Jesus in the Early Church* (Edinburgh: T. & T. Clark, 1990).

110 *"This day the Eden":* Toal, *Sunday Sermons,* vol. IV, 427.

111 *"So it was fitting":* Ibid., 434.

111 *"What honors":* Ibid., 429.

112 *the Church gives her honor:* On the distinction between veneration of the Virgin and adoration of God, see the *Catechism of the Catholic Church,* no. 971. The Second

Vatican Council, in *Lumen Gentium* 66, clarified the unique veneration given to Mary (as distinct from other saints) and the unique worship offered to God: "Mary is rightly honored by a special cult [*hyperdoulia*] in the Church. . . . This cult, . . . for all its uniqueness, differs essentially from the cult of adoration, which is offered equally to the Incarnate Word, and to the Father, and to the Holy Spirit." This outlook is reflected in Saint Epiphanius's condemnation of the ancient Collyridian heresy, which held that the eucharistic sacrifice could be offered *to* Mary.

117 *"God paid such honor": Oration Concerning Simeon and Anna* 5.

118 *Pope Leo the Great: On the Nativity,* Sermon 6.

119 *"The Son of God became a son":* Athanasius, *On the Incarnation of the Word of God* 8. On the centrality of deification and divine filiation in Catholic soteriology, see A. N. Williams, *The Ground of Union: Deification in Aquinas and Palamas* (New York: Oxford University Press, 1999); Francis Fernandez-Carvajal and Peter Beteta, *Children of God* (Princeton, N.J.: Scepter Publishers, 1997); Paul Wadell, *Friends of God: Virtues and Gifts in*

Aquinas (New York: Peter Lang, 1991); Romanus Cessario, *The Godly Image: Christ and Salvation in Catholic Thought from Anselm to Aquinas* (Petersham, Mass.: St. Bede's Publications, 1990).

120 *Council of Trent: Denzinger* 796.

121 *Pope John Paul II:* Postsynodal apostolic exhortation *Christifideles Laici* 11.3 (1988).

121 *"All men are one man":* Augustine, *On Psalm 39* 2.

122 *"For is not Mary the Mother":* Pius X, encyclical letter *Ad Diem Illum* 10 (1904).

127 *"maternal mediation":* See Pope John Paul II, *Theotokos: Woman, Mother, Disciple* (Boston: Pauline Books, 2000), 236–43.

129 *"Original sin attempts":* Pope John Paul II, *Crossing the Threshold of Hope* (New York: Alfred A. Knopf, 1994), 228.

140 On Mary as archetype of the Church, see Pope John Paul II, *Theotokos,* 218; Ignace de la Potterie, S.J., *Mary in*

the Mystery of the Covenant (Staten Island, N.Y.: Alba House, 1992); Otto Semmelroth, S.J., *Mary Archetype of the Church* (New York: Sheed and Ward, 1963).

140 *In fact, the Marian teaching:* See William G. Most, *Vatican II—Marian Council* (Athlone, Ireland: Alba House, 1972).

143 *"by the power of the Holy Spirit":* On the close and profound correlation of divine maternity in the Holy Spirit, Mary (as icon or creaturely replica), and the Church, see John Milbank, *The Word Made Strange: Theology, Language, Culture* (Oxford: Basil Blackwell, 1997), 172–93; Paul Evdokimov, *Woman and the Salvation of the World* (Crestwood, N.Y.: St. Vladimir's Seminary Press 1994), 189–225; F. X. Durrwell, *Mary: Icon of the Spirit and of the Church* (London: St. Paul Publications, 1991), 17–73; idem, *Holy Spirit of God* (London: Geoffrey Chapman, 1986), 107–59; H. Manteau-Bonamy, O.P., *The Immaculate Conception and the Holy Spirit: The Marian Teaching of Maximilian Kolbe* (San Francisco: Ignatius Press, 1988); Barbara Albrecht, "Is There an Objective Type, 'Woman'?" in Joseph Ratzinger et al., eds., *The Church and Women* (San Francisco: Ignatius Press, 1988),

35–49; André Feuillet, *Jesus and His Mother: The Role of the Virgin Mary in Salvation History and the Place of Woman in the Church* (Still River, Mass.: St. Bede's Publications, 1984), 192–212; Joseph Cardinal Ratzinger, *Daughter Zion* (San Francisco: Ignatius Press, 1983), 25–27; Yves Congar, O.P., *I Believe in the Holy Spirit,* vol. 3 (New York: Seabury Press, 1983), 155–64; Louis Bouyer, *The Church of God* (Chicago: Franciscan Herald Press, 1982), 540–44; idem, *The Seat of Wisdom* (New York: Pantheon Books, 1962), 175–90; Scheeben, *The Mysteries of Christianity,* 181–90.

145 *impediment to Christian unity:* For a sampling of the many significant works on Mary by Protestant scholars, growing out of the modern ecumenical movement, see W. McLoughlin and J. Pinnock, eds., *Mary Is for Everyone: Essays on Mary and Ecumenism* (Wiltshire: Cromwell Press, 1997); Charles Dickson, *A Protestant Pastor Looks at Mary* (Huntington, Ind.: Our Sunday Visitor, 1996); John Macquarrie, *Mary for All Christians* (Grand Rapids, Mich.: Eerdmans, 1990); A. Stacpoole, ed., *Mary's Place in Christian Dialogue* (Wilton, Conn.: Morehouse-Barlow, 1982); John de Satge, *Down to Earth: The New Protestant Vision of the Virgin Mary* (London: SPCK, 1976); Stephen Benko, *Protestants, Catholics, and Mary* (Valley Forge, Pa.:

Judson Press, 1968); Max Thurian, *Mary, Mother of All Christians* (New York: Herder and Herder, 1964).

166 *In its official documents:* See, for example, Joseph P. Christopher, ed., *The Raccolta* (New York: Benziger Brothers, 1943), no. 360.

170 *Anne Winston-Allen:* "The Remaking of the Rosary," *New Covenant*, October 1998, 14, and *Stories of the Rose* (State College, Pa.: Pennsylvania State University Press, 1997).

PHOTO COURTESY OF LEGATUS

SCOTT HAHN is professor of theology and Scripture at the Franciscan University of Steubenville and was recently appointed to the Pope Benedict XVI Chair of Biblical Theology and Liturgical Proclamation at Saint Vincent Seminary. He is the author of more than a dozen books, including *The Lamb's Supper; Hail, Holy Queen; Swear to God;* and *Understanding the Scriptures.* Dr. Hahn is also Founder and President of the St. Paul Center for Biblical Theology, located in Steubenville, Ohio, where he lives with his wife, Kimberly, and their six children.